OWN YOUR
AUTHORITY

OWN YOUR
AUTHORITY

FOLLOW YOUR INSTINCTS, RADIATE CONFIDENCE, AND COMMUNICATE AS A LEADER PEOPLE TRUST

MARISA SANTORO

NEW YORK   CHICAGO   SAN FRANCISCO   ATHENS   LONDON
MADRID   MEXICO CITY   MILAN   NEW DELHI
SINGAPORE   SYDNEY   TORONTO

1 2 3 4 5 6 7 8 9   LCR   26 25 24 23 22 21

ISBN   978-1-264-25816-1
MHID   1-264-25816-X

e-ISBN   978-1-264-25817-8
e-MHID   1-264-25817-8

Library of Congress Cataloging-in-Publication Data

Names: Santoro, Marisa, author.
Title: Own your authority : follow your instincts, radiate confidence, and
   communicate as a leader people trust / Marisa Santoro.
Description: New York : McGraw Hill, [2021] | Includes bibliographical references
   and index.
Identifiers: LCCN 2020055475 (print) | LCCN 2020055476 (ebook) |
   ISBN 9781264258161 (hardback) | ISBN 9781264258178 (ebook)
Subjects: LCSH: Leadership. | Self-confidence. | Authority. | Trust. | Success in
   business.
Classification: LCC HD57.7 .S266 2021 (print) | LCC HD57.7 (ebook) |
   DDC 658.4/092—dc23
LC record available at https://lccn.loc.gov/2020055475
LC ebook record available at https://lccn.loc.gov/2020055476

For my mom:
"Shoot for the moon,
even if you land among the stars."
I'm still listening.

Every time you have to speak,
you are auditioning for leadership.
JAMES HUMES

CONTENTS

ACKNOWLEDGMENTS

The following relationships have been placed on my path, and for that I am forever grateful.

To my family who has always believed in me and helped me define the gutsy leader vision. Vince, for his loving patience and giving me so much of that precious resource called time. To my children, for all those tight hugs and never complaining about the late nights Mom was working. To my sister and brothers: Eva, Joe, and John—thank you for always cheering me on and keeping my feet planted in our Brooklyn roots. You were my first readers and biggest fans. I have never forgotten your encouragement. To my nephew John, whose support has always been one phone call away.

To Joe, my mentor and dear friend. Without your belief and investment in me early on, this work would not have been possible.

To Gordon, your inspiring words of wisdom were priceless. Thank you so much for supporting me when this work was just a seed of an idea. Our partnership was a divinely timed gutsy move.

To Helena, Diane, and Jo, thank you for your years of friendship. You were always listening even when I wasn't speaking. I am truly blessed to have such strong, wise women on my team.

To my sister spirit, Cyndi—thank you for your constant encouragement and for always holding space for me in celebration.

To Sarah—all those marvelous Monday mornings coast-to-coast with you have made all the difference. Thank you for your creative input and honest feedback.

To Annette, Angela, Megan, and Joann, thank you for contributing your time and believing in my mission to pay it forward. Your support has spoken volumes. To Harold, who unknowingly sparked my reconnection to writing again.

To the In Our Shoes community and gutsy leader village—thank you all for allowing me into your lives and trusting me with your greater vision.

To Jack Canfield and Steve Harrison, your guidance has been priceless—thank you for everything.

Special thanks to Grace Freedson, who stood behind this work from the start and whose trusted guidance never steered me wrong to see it to fruition. To Amy Li and her star team along with everyone at McGraw Hill—from designers to marketing—who championed this book and worked alongside me every step of the way to make it possible. Thank you so much. To Patty Wallenburg and her team, who left no stone unturned during production. Your professionalism and guidance were sincerely appreciated.

To Grace—thank you for all those gutsy whispers that I could no longer ignore.

OWN YOUR
AUTHORITY

INTRODUCTION

If you are a confident professional
who knows your own value, that's not enough.
Are you always projecting that you are?
Are you always weaving it in?

There's plenty of professional advice offering what to *do* to be successful in your career, but there's not much talk around who to *be* and how to show up intuitively listening to what's not placed directly in front of you. You won't find guidance on leadership sourced from no more than a hunch. If it's not stimulated by one of the five senses, it gets swept under the rug. In the pursuit of effective leadership, more attention has been given to rational decision making over a slow, reflective approach that places trust in instinct. However, as you build confidence and begin to trust your gut, you become more nimble as a decision maker.

Business psychology offers emotional intelligence to help raise the self-awareness antennas, but how does one practically apply this feel-good concept to one's career and truly accelerate? Intelligent, hard-working professionals are wired for growth and to consistently keep learning. They want to know how to reach their desired level of leadership, and they want to do it with a boldness that feels authentic and is aligned with their true nature.

Reaching a leadership position in any career is a marker of success, but passionate leaders seeking to make a high impact in their field crave no spotlight and seek no glamour. If you're reading this book, chances are that you are that kind of leader. You revel in deep, one-on-one, meaningful conversations before seeking to win friends and influence people. Your education, skills, and experience may have helped you make it through the door; yet there are still moments when you stand frozen. You may feel entirely confident about your grasp of your subject matter and expertise; yet you still want to instinctively know what to say and do without feeling stuck in perfection paralysis mode when making yourself visible. You want the bold moves to find voice in your statements but without the self-doubt that tags along when you stick your neck out a little. You want to walk into any conversation, self-promote naturally, and sell your ideas, projecting confidence with a guaranteed commitment to deliver on the results you promise.

How can you consistently maintain your value and relevance as you grow as a leader? How can you find the freedom to throw away the script and confidently lead, knowing who you are at your core when you face off with senior management while harboring a fear of failure? How can you go from the relied-on, behind-the-scenes subject matter expert to strategic thinker and voice an opinion that goes against the grain of conventional thought in the room? How do you show some emotion and still become a respected leader whom people trust? None of these are possible without allowing yourself to trust your gut to make decisions that give you the freedom to move forward.

TRUSTING YOUR INSTINCTS AND HAVING CLEAR COMMUNICATION ARE BOLD MOVES

Having a strong sense of self naturally qualifies us to inspire and influence others, but this can also come at a price. You can end up overprojecting that calm and confident presence to avoid looking like a pushover, but trying to take on an unemotional, slightly harder personality can result in a feeling of disconnect as to who you really are. In contrast, sitting on your hands and waiting to be picked offers a "no-guts, no-glory" sense of resignation. The more passion and energy you bring to a conversation in your authentic way, the more you intuitively communicate and "tap into" others' needs and thought processes.

Trusting your gut plays a key role in being present to the person you are while achieving your goals. But you may not pay much mind to your gut feelings because they're not tangible and are quickly shot down by your ego, whose sole purpose is to keep you safe and sound: "Whoa, hang on! You're way too assertive today. Who do you think you are attempting to acquire happiness and success?" Inspired instinctual action can bring out the hunter in you, along with the feeling of being in motion that can evoke a sense of progress that allows you to stay the course toward any breakthrough goal.

The instinctive mind is a feeling, not a tangible roadmap. The purpose of this book is to offer you a strategic blueprint to lead with influence and to combine your authentic personality with your years of experience and skill sets that speak for themselves and stand on their own. Whether you're just one year into your career or a veteran of two decades, the *gutsy leader* roadmap laid out here *works*. This is instinctive leadership that creates mindful, responsive energy. It is not forceful or driven by emotional knee-jerk reactions. When you resort to such emotional reactions, you too easily give away your power, which, in turn, can cause you to retreat when faced with challenges. You can also be perceived as a leader who has little patience and becomes easily irritated. The result is that you subtly show up as being reclusive, procrastinating, or avoiding potential conflict.

Words matter. I am not just referring to what you say to others in the form of body language, emails, presentations, casual chitchat, or formal discussions but, more important, what you say to yourself first and on a regular basis. Successful business leaders speak up with clear communication and thrive by taking on measured risk. They tackle some form of daily discomfort through a focus on both internal and external dialogue to achieve higher levels of influence and leadership. Success in any area of life, whether in your career, relationships, health, or finances, rarely exceeds personal development, and this is why personal development is critical to your continued growth. Rest assured, this path gets easier over time when you're willing to be comfortable being *uncomfortable*. The success system defined in this book invites you to embrace your instincts as much as your knowledge and experience and will work in any area of your life, not just your career. Following your instincts develops self-trust and just happens to have the power to change your life.

> *By "guts" I mean, grace under pressure.*
> ERNEST HEMINGWAY

GUTSY TODAY, BOLDER TOMORROW

The primary reason we don't allow ourselves to be guided by our intuition is three primary human fears: the fear of failure, the fear of rejection, and the fear of looking foolish. Fears show up as repeating patterns that have been hardwired into us since childhood. Although we may be aware of our personal roadblocks, we don't always act on them right away when we find ourselves in the eye of a storm. We become too caught up resisting when instead we should be calmly taking a step back with faith and turning that difficult circumstance swiftly around *on our own terms*.

Clarity is power. The more you listen to your intuition, the easier it becomes to be assertive about what you want. This is the heart of increasing your confidence in any area—taking on risk in small increments, stepping into new territory, facing fears, learning, failing, growing, and circling back to take on more risk that will stretch but not freeze you. This is how you build a rock-solid brand and foundation to fall back on and fail forward from. You don't learn from taking cliffside jumps overnight. You learn from working a slow and steady muscle that acts on instinct, gaining practical experience from increased self-trust over time.

Companies globally have made leadership cultivation a top-level initiative by injecting training and development programs into their operations. Yet one thing is still lacking in traditional learning approaches. They miss the mark on the self-leadership component and the transformation that professionals make when they recognize how they see themselves first *and* how they relate to others. Going through every prerequisite stage of obtaining the right skills, adapting to company culture, confirming a clear understanding of business drivers, and passing all the examinations and certifications is essential. Still, this kind of leadership development goes beyond checking the right boxes, or attempting to fit into a box someone else has defined for you. You can always ramp up and learn the skills you need to be relevant in your career, but without the mindset to *be* in your true skin and course-correct your growth path, that training quickly becomes "shelf help" that is lost and ineffective. Understanding who you are, your beliefs, and your emotions, as well as their effect on others, is the root that will ground you, especially when tough talks and decisions need to happen.

Leadership cultivation motivates and empowers professionals by creating a supportive environment where recognition for results is at the forefront, irrespective of whether or not one fits the mold of current leaders. This then raises the question: Should the next generation of leaders look and feel like current leadership? The answer is *no*. Expecting diverse talent to conform defeats the purpose of all diversity and inclusion initiatives.[1] From an economic perspective, organizations and countries which tap into diverse talent pools are stronger.

How Can I Be Sure That I Am Following My Instinct and Not Reacting to My Own Anxiety When I Make a Decision?

Have you ever felt excited and nervous at the same time? When these two emotions coexist, that's your intuition speaking, and it will never steer you wrong. The best move for you is never rooted in fear. Instead, it's rooted in where these two emotions coexist. If you are ever unsure, close your eyes. You should feel a calm sense of knowing from your core despite any chatter of self-doubt that attempts to rationalize your decision away. Still waters run deep—"beneath a placid exterior hides a passionate or subtle nature."[2]

ATTENTION IS INTENTION

At In Our Shoes, a career leadership training and career coaching practice based in the New York City area, a *gutsy move* is defined as an impulse to act conceived when a call to action feels uncomfortable. You are nervous yet at the same time excited for the growth that lies ahead. When you have a positive expectation without being tied to a fixed outcome of how it will unfold, you are in a high-intention, low-attachment state. Needing to control how something turns out based on your actions keeps you in a holding pattern where no progress can be made. However, when you are intentional about the direction in which you want to move, holding onto the positive feeling attached to your decision, that's when you can trust yourself. True freedom is letting go of the need to control the conditions under which you create successful outcomes.

Most people who put in the work have a hard time letting go, only to remain distressed afterward. This happens when they are clinging to a need to control the outcome, showing up in a high-intention, high-attachment state instead. This is not using your instinct to your advantage. You only accelerate growth when you're willing to take on some calculated risk and trust yourself fueled by your positive intention. Such bold moves strengthen and become more impactful over time. When you cocreate what you want with your intuition, you begin to see new and different outcomes for the same old circumstances, which in their heyday used to drag you down. When you spend a few times each day reflecting and focusing on what you want—that bigger vision—you define success on your own terms.

What if we channeled our inner energy in such a way that we could tap into an area of growth, which would be a welcome stretch instead of an intimidating iceberg that freezes us? This book pivots career leadership on its head and splits it into two simple how-to categories: (1) raise the volume on your internal dialogue, guiding you to higher levels of self-awareness and new opportunities, to become a credible leader whom people trust and (2) take action vis-à-vis your bold moves when the intuitive hits arrive.

KNOW THYSELF LEADERSHIP

Becoming an instinctive leader begins with developing a sense of who you are: What makes you tick? What are your beliefs? How do you relate to others? And how do you respond in those relationships? While many people agree that following one's gut instinct can lead to success in business or any other area of life, they're not convinced that they were necessarily born with an ability to truly follow their hunches and trust themselves. Consider this: planning our days is important. We can't operate in this life without the structure that comes with a schedule. But plans will also always ellude us. When was the last time something didn't go according to plan for you? Did you move past it? I'm willing to bet that you adjusted your plans and rerouted. This is an example of your instinct taking charge.

This natural instinct of yours is more "visibly" present in your life than anything you have experienced materially and is consistently being channeled through your interactions with people (often perfect strangers), places, and things that present themselves to you every day. While you may fundamentally believe in your self-worth and career potential, there's also an "inner crow" feeding into your limiting beliefs, kicking to the curb those momentary impulses to take action. This book will inspire you to turn those moments of self-doubt around to create positive actions on your terms. You will no longer ask for permission to move ahead in your career but instead "go with your gut" and step into that higher version and vision of yourself as an influencer. This book will show how you can show up as a bold leader with grace and ease.

WHY WE NEED MORE
AUTHENTIC BOLD LEADERS

> When we consistently rely on and act from instinct, we are more confident
> in our decisions as leaders and better able to sell our ideas authentically.
> Leading from our gut, we will own our authority every time and self-qualify
> as experts in our field, moving past any limiting beliefs and negative
> environments. In doing so, we also embrace self-love and compassion,
> which increase our mental game and health.

In a world that marches to the drumbeats of truth and transparency, the bar could not be set higher for leaders today. The demand has shifted, calling for leadership that does more than just deliver on bottom-line results but that is passionately driven from the bottom up. There is a louder cry now to nurture human relationships and operate from a place of service in value-driven organizations by putting employees before the customers to attract more customers.

This book is directed toward mindful, hardworking professionals who are lifelong learners and wired to thrive with a growth mindset. Once these professionals have clarity around the direction they wish to go in their careers, they won't hold back and will work backward doing whatever it takes, led by their instinctive roadmap.

Nothing in life is definite, so how can we truly know when making major career decisions that they will always be in our best interest? This includes trusting the people we allow to enter our lives. How do we know when to trust our instinct when it screams against the grain of popular opinion?

This book answers this question and lays out a step-by-step blueprint on how you can discover your bold moves aligned with your personal style without resorting to aggressive behavior or losing your composure. The more you speak up across all areas of your life, the more successful you will become.

Your intuitive voice is not meant to trigger the red siren alerts directing you on which path to take. It's deliberately placed quietly in your core as barely a whisper for you to tune into, with free will to discover that next best choice for you. If there were any prerequisites to making this system work like clockwork, then it would be one thing: you have to be willing to tune out the noise around you and listen to what lies beyond the five senses, stepping head-on into fear. You have to be willing to commit to yourself by following your truth despite what you see in front of you.

GUTSY LIVING

Gutsy leadership is a lifestyle change that can be applied to any area of your life—how you build strong relationships with your family, living in the house of your dreams, or building financial wealth. It's a muscle you work every day until using it becomes as natural as breathing. Challenges eventually get swept to the side to make way for glowing opportunities waiting around the corner that are fully aligned with what you need but not always with what you want. The caveat is that you have to ask and do so with confident conviction. You have to be willing to become a reverse paranoid and curiously ask, "How is this problem helping me grow?"—and you have to be willing to be led.

> A daily reminder, in case you forgot what you stand for: you don't get up in the morning to blend in with everyone else.

The leadership success principles in this book are based on my two decades of going from survive to thrive mode, consistently advancing as a woman working in a male-dominated career and industry. It is also based on my career experiences from years of coaching professionals who come from diverse industries and expert fields. You will find the answers to their most frequently asked questions throughout this book that cover work scenarios that you, too, may be experiencing *in your shoes*. This isn't just about your career. This system works in any area of your life, in and outside of work.

As a bold leader, you are either an intrapreneur working for an organization or an entrepreneur running a business. In both positions, you have clients. Your managers, peers, team, and business partners are all your clients. The mindset shifts you make will drive your career growth and increase your "sticker value" by first shifting how you see yourself which in turn shifts how you are perceived as an expert in your field. The ripple effect from this journey is that you will inevitably support other professionals as well. These are the people who work with you and who, through your example, will also lead with influence simply from your inspiration.

Gutsy leadership is a paradigm shift in the way professionals can develop as leaders of influence through a focus on mindset and intuition to push beyond their limits. It implores an inside-out self-leadership approach to recognize your *why*—what motivates you and how you relate to others, including an effort to learn what makes them tick as well. This is how you authentically drive change and lead with influence. You don't have to sell anyone on you. That inner belief in yourself first is what moves and encourages others to trust in you. It works whether you are just starting out in your career, at midcareer, or in a senior executive role. It also works if you are exploring a career transition or have a business and stand behind the value your company delivers.

Professionals often ask why they feel confident in their expertise but not always confident in how they show up in their business relationships or in certain work interactions. If this sounds like you, you are not alone. When you are clear on your value and the results you are promising, that's when you lock in a core belief in yourself that is felt throughout any conversation you have.

An important question to answer is, "How do I want to be perceived?" The answer to this question will dictate how others respond to you and support your intention wherever you go. When you are clear about who you are, others will be too, and they will place their trust in you.

Today there is still primarily a focus on dynamic energy—what we need to *do* to achieve personal and professional success—versus silent mindful energy, which drives who we need to *be*. We often measure success and productivity with the tangible—things that we can see, hear, feel, taste, and touch physically. In the public conversation, this accounts for 99 percent of how success is measured, whereas instinct accounts for only 1 percent. If global economies are to develop more leaders of influence on their playing fields, then change has to happen on two fronts: professionals need to change the images of how they see themselves, and businesses need to change how they define the success of their employees.

The leadership approach laid out here comes down to a simple formula: when you consistently rely on and act from intuition, with a positive expectation of your results, you will trust yourself, take on more risk, make better decisions, become more confident from successful decision making, build more influence, and therefore sell your ideas to more people.

Here's the catch: developing the skills to be a leader doesn't happen immediately. Although we may understand this, we don't always allow ourselves to take the necessary time we need. We convince ourselves that we have to figure it all out on day one and drink from the fire hose to have all the answers. However, clarity and confidence in your decisions build over time. Over time, you will learn to trust your instinct just like any muscle in your body.

When you commit to staying the course led by your intuitive guidance system, you begin to take on bolder actions that are directly related to your risk tolerance at that time. Be good to yourself: you will grow this strength steadily. Consider a goal that you believe has the power to change your life positively. If it hasn't happened yet, then there is something that you are not willing to risk in the process of creating it. Every goal comes with some level of risk. You may not want to risk a comfortable and flexible lifestyle by transitioning to a new leadership role. You may not want to risk having the stress that comes from making a higher income or managing a team. Failure comes with risk. It's when you learn from failure that you succeed.

You can measure opportunity with the same yardstick
that measures the risk involved. They go together.
EARL NIGHTINGALE

Gutsy leadership is not only having the self-awareness to know when you are opting in but also being fully aware of when you are quietly opting out. In silence, you speak volumes. This very much contrasts with the knee-jerk reaction to throw your chips in, write the resignation letter, and walk away because you are one inch away from a mental breakdown. Instead, professionals should be addressing the subtle retreats they make by giving away their power in everyday situations—remaining silent, not piping up in meetings, allowing others to take credit for their ideas, and allowing top-down management styles and abusive senior power in order to protect their own jobs at the expense of their team.

It's nonnegotiable to lead from your gut if you take yourself seriously in your field. Your gutsy moves are bursting at the seams in the very moment when you are wincing from pain and distress. This is when you are given a choice—the choice to act swiftly when the instinctual hits arrive, the choice to trust yourself.

The opposite to courage is not cowardice.
The opposite to courage is conformity.
ROLLO MAY

DON'T THINK. JUST GO

So what if you don't want to take a risk in your career and are comfortable where you are? In the end, it's a choice but still a responsibility to lean into those everyday discomforts before you reach that breaking point in case you do want to grow later on. Nip this in the bud. Think of this as a game of chess where the events slamming you down are no more than a distraction to keep you from playing bigger. This is a key mindset shift to make: embrace conflict rather than avoid or resist it because you understand that conflict is there for a reason. You are always being called to step up and grow through each conflict, whether you consciously caused it to happen or not. Conflicts are placed in your path for a reason and often surface based on different circumstances but always at the root of the same desire—you are being called to expand. When you feel those intuitive hits (referred to as *downloads* from intuition, spirit, and that sixth sense in the In Our Shoes community), assess the risks and place your stake in the ground as you address the situation head-on. It's important to make sure that this action isn't something that feels like a super stretch that will freeze you. Act on instinct right away, and don't question it. Our Achilles' heel is overthinking and analyzing everything beforehand versus just pressing "Go." This isn't to say that you never need to analyze your thoughts before acting on them. However, if you have a thought and it feels so aligned with who you are and where you are in life, then *act on it.*

If you are not waking up each morning willing to get your hands dirty and take on some level of calculated risk (which, by definition, must go against the popular grain), then you are not feeding your soul, which is meant to consistently expand. Opting out is simply not an option. You can feel bigger and better things waiting just around the bend, namely being the leader of influence you believe you can be. The choice is yours. Do you sit on your hands and settle for where you are now, or do you make some bold moves that will expand you and, likely, risk a few fumbles? Our world is expanding and therefore so are you.

You may be intelligent, educated, and confident, but that doesn't always mean that you are being perceived that way. If you know that you are strong but aren't always projecting that you are, then this book was written for you. You will question your confidence the moment any self-doubt creeps in. Being clear about what you deliver and why your clients need your value self-qualifies you to be in that new desired role. This is what makes a bold leader of influence.

This book is meant to pull you up toward fulfillment as a business leader by slaying the conversations in your mind that are negatively affecting your confidence level and the decisions you make. Once you can overcome those self-limiting beliefs, you are free to compete in any arena in which you want to lead.

It takes seconds to convince yourself that you will fail, that you are not good enough, or that your track record may not measure up to transition to a new level, role, or career. I've been in all those shoes. If we're honest, it's not too hard to say, "Well, if it hasn't happened yet, it never will." Does this sound familiar? When this happens, take a step back, removing the need to have a fixed how-to path laid out. Have faith that you have what it takes to advance, get unstuck, and become visible and excited about all that you have to offer. Honor the questions you ask yourself that challenge the status quo; they are instinctual and never random.

This book is based on practical experience and how-to advice on becoming a leader in your industry. It's locking in who you are and what your intention is and then wrapping clarity and communication around that intention so that others become so clear on your *why* that they can no longer ignore you. This is a nonnegotiable way to show up in your career if you want to keep growing. It's a shift from pushing hard and *doing* all the time to pulling in great things by *being* your authentic self. It's acting when your gut voices an enthusiastic *yes* even when it sounds like a whisper. It's acting on the intuitive hits that say "Go. Now" without questioning and being open to possibility versus heading home, talking yourself out of that which felt right for you only a few hours earlier.

This kind of bold leadership is not for the faint of heart. It's for those who have struggled with selling themselves and making small talk. It's for those who are not articulating what they want and need in their career and want to manage conflict easier and be seen as a valued strategic leader doing impactful work. It's for professionals who feel isolated without a solid senior-level network to rely on for opportunities. It's for those who are producing results with high impact but little return and recognition. It's for those who are afraid that they may never be able to achieve a successful career or have work-life balance. It's especially for those who have achieved success but are not "owning" where they are despite their success. This book will give you permission to ask for what you need, where perhaps you have always taken care of others first, putting their priorities above yours.

As a daily habit, I invite you to reflect and ask yourself, "Did I give myself the *yes* today? Did I make things happen? Did I follow my gut?" This consistent self-assessment is what develops your personal power and is a prerequisite to lead and influence others.

1

SELF-PROMOTE WITH EASE AND AUTHENTICITY

LET YOUR RESULTS DO THE TALKING

Public speaking (regardless of audience size) is an activity that most people fear. Many successful business leaders share that they still have stomach jitters right before getting behind a microphone. The most successful speakers admit that there is always that flicker of self-doubt and fear of acceptance. Virgin founder Richard Branson openly admits that despite his very spotlight public image, he was always terrified of public speaking and still is. Through the power of visualization, he walks himself through speaking engagements weeks beforehand. He rehearses in his living room to create what appears to be an impromptu performance, even though he practices repeatedly until he reaches his fear-free comfort level. He became so successful at using visualization as a technique to overcome the anxiety, that he began teaching courses on the art of public speaking. His best advice to contain your nerves is to pretend that you are speaking to just one person, not a room full of people, and practice, practice, practice! Both of these techniques will help you feel more natural over time.

Let's imagine a scenario where you are suddenly asked to speak to an audience about your accomplishments and what you are most proud of. Self-promoting comes with a one-two punch in terms of the fear barometer. Not only can it make you want to crawl under the table to avoid being put on the spot, but it also delivers the kind of anxiety that can feel as though you are no longer breathing. Would this impromptu exercise be easy for you, or would you get so caught up in how you are being scrutinized and judged that you would likely freeze and want to retreat?

If the latter, let's strip down this one fear, because conquering it is a gutsy move that comes with big payoffs. In this scenario, you could share what you have enjoyed doing in your career and what you have learned. You can also share your passion genuinely and show where your work has made a significant positive impact on both your career and your life.

Reality check—it's highly unlikely that you would ever find yourself in this type of spotlight pressure situation, but I'd like you to consider it anyway. If you consider yourself a professional subject matter expert who wants your results and reputation to be taken seriously, then I invite you to become *very* comfortable in self-promotion mode. Taking it one step further, I want you to consider waking up every day and acting as if you were dropped into a chair and asked to talk about one thing—your value. This isn't selling yourself but, in fact, *being* yourself. If you consider yourself a growth-minded professional who wants your results and reputation to be taken seriously, then it's a nonnegotiable to talk about your best work with enthusiasm because that's an energy that people *feel*. I guarantee that you would know instinctively precisely what to say. This isn't winging it. When you trust your gut, the words will always come.

Statistically, your next opportunity will likely not come from a friend or family member. Your next opportunity may come from an acquaintance whom you met at a conference, a colleague or business partner at an internal company event, or possibly even a referred contact. As any sales leader will share, a 100 percent referral business is a self-sustaining business model that, in the long run, will sell itself. Your audience will remember you for years to come—not necessarily for your work per se but for how you made them feel. It's the *feeling* that people remember. Self-promotion creates that experience.

If you don't communicate your value, why would you expect anyone else to? Why would you expect anyone to refer you on?

Although it may not be your typical day-to-day reality, act *as if* you are speaking to an audience in even the smallest of meeting venues. Visualize a microphone in front of you at all times. This leadership principle applies whether you are having a one-on-one discussion or speaking to a large room. People are waiting to learn from you. Before you enter into any conversation, consider how you want your audience to feel by the time you close. The more included you make people feel in that setting, the more open-eared and accepting they will be to *listen* to what you have to say from your self-created platform of authority. Inclusive leaders steer discussions in a direction they instinctively feel can benefit the collective tide. Such leaders share their thoughts and ideas in order to stimulate innovative ideas in others, namely their teams.

Building your personal brand is much like building the frame of a home. Your personal brand showcases the *results* you deliver and the leadership assets you bring to the table. When you know your brand, you can, at any given moment, speak calmly about what your experience brings and talk about why clients should buy into your products and how they will benefit. Personal brand is also often referred to as your *unique value proposition*.

Owning your unique value is based on a three-part formula. The first part is having *clarity* on your expertise, skills, and the things for which you have been commended over time—that which you have accomplished. This also includes your natural talents and behaviors that have helped you establish a name for yourself, such as having an empathic nature or holding strong to ethical practices.

The second way for you to own your unique value involves being clear on your *results* and what you deliver to your clients. Your clients are your business partners, management, peers, and direct reports. Everyone is your client.

The third component to owning your value is leading with your authentic personality and leveraging your personal charm factor. Many leaders share that they don't always feel that they can be completely authentic or are sometimes too cautious and hide behind formality instead of using their natural ability to show their true selves and listen and relate to others. These are natural human skills that support your ability to lead with influence.

Breaking this down further, knowing your core expertise increases your clarity and confidence as a leader. Being clear on the results you have achieved for your clients helps you to communicate effectively and market your value to the right people. Leading with your authentic personality increases your connection with others.

Whether you are an intrapreneur working for an organization or an entrepreneur working for yourself, everyone has clients. People want promises. People want to believe what you believe as long as they can envision how your results will benefit *them*—that's when they will buy into you and when you know you are marketing yourself genuinely.

Be comfortable with being uncomfortable. Self-promotion initially doesn't feel easy or natural. However, the more you allow yourself to be uncomfortable, the more you will find yourself taking low-level risks over time. This, in turn, builds confidence that steadily supports a trust in yourself and in your instincts—and the cycle repeats from there. More self-trust leads to taking more risks and a willingness to do what comes instinctively. When this self-trust is guided by those you serve, it leads to more people placing their trust in you and your team's results. This leads to more confidence in your work, thereby increasing your influence.

Let's unpack this further. Let's say that you are a manufacturer of hand tools, and your company sells saws. Rather than diving into all the bells and whistles you make available, such as the different types of blades your customers can swap in and out, you should focus instead on how your saw is going to make your customers' lives easier. Your marketing might also highlight how much time your customers will save, promising that they can slice through any piece of wood in under three minutes and that this will save them hundreds of dollars if they have to pay for hired help. This is what I mean by your personal brand—leveraging your authentic personality, standing behind your product's expert function, and promising results.

Whether you are speaking on a phone call, sitting with a team, or making a presentation to a board of directors, you are always advocating for yourself. Your message should be broadcast clearly enough that any audience can relate to what you are saying. This is a mindset shift that many leaders struggle with. In other words, when you are self-promoting your project, your idea, your achievements, your team's performance, your vision, or whatever your message, act *as if* the whole world is a stage, because it is. We understand this today through the power of technology—one uttered word of wisdom or content-rich video can be shared globally in seconds, ensuring that your message and trusted reputation stick.

By managing the perception at that moment, your goal is to leave your listeners wanting more and able to take you home with them. When people take you home with them, they leave saying the speaker had some great advice to share today that supported me. "He [or she] made some good points I hadn't considered. I'm going to share that guidance with others who can also benefit from those words of wisdom." Through the quality of your message, now you are being referred on as an expert in your field and a leader of influence.

Genuine leaders are not there to speak for the sake of speaking. When they speak, they lock their listeners in with their *why*—why they have set the direction of an initiative, why their teams consist of the resident professional experts. This is what makes a leader of influence, and you do this with a "go-giving" as opposed to a "go-gaining" mentality. Go-giving leaders leverage their authority to empower their teams and clients and create a sense of shared commitment in their message, rather than assuming control because of their very position of power. This insight can only be gained by understanding what it's like to be in your client's shoes. Go-gaining on the other hand is increasing influence for the sole purpose of advancing your own agenda and career irrespective of what impact your actions have on others.

According to Bob Burg, coauthor of the *Go-Giver* book series, the essence of influence is pull; that as opposed to push. Pushing is trying to lead or influence others through compliance . . . or some type of coercion. It's attempting to control others.

Pull—on the other hand—is an attraction. Successful influencers attract people first to their ideas and then to themselves. Pull results in commitment; in people going out of their way to make sure the job is done right; accomplished to the very best of their ability.

When you consider how strong team cultures form, it becomes apparent that they develop around leaders who take the time to talk about the *why* with their staff. Why are we doing this? Why does this project matter? Why would our clients benefit, and why would this decision be impactful in the long term?

Speaking to your *why* comes before communicating business goals, which are your *what*. Once your goals are understood, then, with sleeves rolled up, you can speak to your *how*. How will this project happen? How will we achieve success? However, you can't reach the *how* and speak to a strategic plan your team can execute unless you start with your *why*.

Your ego plays a strong role in how well you advocate for yourself and the energy that you bring to a conversation to self-advocate effectively. Your ego tries to protect you and keep you small at all times. It's role is to keep you safe. Your growth as a leader occurs when you are able to listen to your ego and still act instinctively anyway despite its desires for self-protection—what is often referred to as the *inner crow*. The first and only conversation that matters is the one you have with yourself, and it is here that self-leadership develops.

Here's how this works on the career front. Assume that you are a subject matter expert leading a given function and are perfectly happy in your current position. Therefore, you may not feel the need to talk about your job or self-promote. One day, however, you may realize that you have become burned out and restless.

This is virtually inevitable because, as humans, we continually seek to learn and grow. You may find yourself in such a situation as a result of any number of events, such as having been passed over for a promotion or receiving a small increase in compensation or insufficient recognition. Irrespective of why, eventually you will want to move on.

Now let's rewind to all your years of playing at leadership but not moving any further into leadership. Your legacy stands on its own, and your ever-competent and proactive nature found ways for your team to work more efficiently and with less time by minimizing manual processes that require human intervention. You may also have replaced outdated processes with more streamlined approaches based on your years of listening closely to the frustrations of your clients sitting in other departments, who were dependent on your team for their own work to be successful. The results you produced for them in the long run made their lives easier.

If I dropped in to interview you on these changes made over time, I'd venture to guess that you could instinctively speak to the positive impact of your leadership. You could tell me how you streamlined workflows and likely boosted productivity, but would you *sell* it to me in that way? Could you talk about it in your sleep so that people in the organization understand how your influence was instrumental to the success of their initiatives?

Whether you alone deserved credit for all those impactful changes or the teams you matrix-managed contributed collectively to the end-to-end process, either way it's your responsibility to talk about your achievements openly. This is nonnegotiable, and here's why: so that you can qualify yourself to go out and advise others on how to do the same following your lead.

Self-promoting is often confused with seeking approval. To the contrary, it is *enjoying* approval, not *needing* it. It's no different from planning the perfect dinner for your family and friends, where you spend hours in the kitchen whipping up the best meal of your life. Hearing those oohs and aahs of culinary satisfaction from your guests at the end of the evening doesn't fill your need to impress others. Cooking for others is a selfless act that psychologically boosts your confidence. It's a "proud me" moment. In just a few hours, you have brought people joy and helped them feel connected to one another, which is what they will remember most about that night—their feel-good emotions.

> *It had long since come to my attention that people*
> *of accomplishment rarely sat back and let things happen*
> *to them. They went out and happened to things.*
> LEONARDO DaVINCI

This is where many leaders tend to get caught up, holding themselves back in their careers. They fall prey to being so comfortable in a particular function or role that they aren't aware of how they would benefit from marketing themselves, speaking of their domain of expertise and of their contributions to the wider organization.

Should this resonate with you too, your knowledge may seem like old news, but there are plenty of others who can learn from you and make further improvements following your lead. You will inevitably also attract people who are drawn to how you think when you're speaking with pride about your work.

When I first broke out of corporate America to pivot into leadership training and coaching, I would never have guessed that my story of exiting to begin a new career was of interest to anyone. Today, the number one question I'm asked before I step off stage is, "How did you go from a 20-year corporate tech career to a leadership coach and trainer?" I began sharing personal stories about the ways I managed my time between my full-time day job and my nighttime "jobby" (a side hustle that feels like a job but is really a hobby) before I felt confident enough to resign. I later developed those backdoor strategies into a formal course that I now deliver in my coaching and training practice. I had never set out to discuss my growth path as a business owner because, at the time, my daily life consisted of self-preservation to keep going emotionally while holding firm to the gutsy leader vision.

You will never know how all the years of blood, sweat, and tears that you've put into your work could be of interest to anyone until someone asks you the question. However, people can't ask the question unless they know about you and your work—which requires marketing yourself. This is the evolution that your career makes from owning your authority and value. Influence is power, not control. It's sharing your thoughts to spark action in others. It's being willing to share your best practices and letting others expand on your ideas to make them even better. What I'm referring to here is your personal and professional impact.

Are You Ready to Own It?

If your answer is *yes* and you are seeking to grow at any stage of your career, then you need to consistently talk about your best work and do it with natural, enthusiastic energy that others can feel. It's the feeling that resonates and the channel through which we instinctively communicate with one another that instills trust.

Rationally, we know that we need to sell ourselves; yet here's the rub: we don't recognize how brilliantly we know how to lead, for no better reason than the fact that we have been doing our jobs for so long as a key player in the process. Worse, we convince ourselves that if we have not transitioned to a more advanced level in our careers, then we are not qualified to talk about the things we know now. We wait for a permission slip from upper management or our clients and peers to speak up. However, the very opposite is true: you self-qualify first by recognizing the skills and experience you have right now. Preparation meets opportunity. As you keep growing in your role and gaining more experience, you continue to talk about what you do well and how it applies to and ultimately benefits others. This is when people straighten up their backs to listen and hear what you have to share. They don't want to hear what you do brilliantly or how you do it. They want to hear your belief in *you*. This is when your influence rises, through the continuous process of authentically promising on what you can deliver until it becomes as natural as breathing.

There is a vicious cycle we can fall into. We tend to think, "I don't know where to start speaking of my accomplishments." I challenge this and ask, "Is that a true statement? Are you taking responsibility for how you are perceived professionally if you choose not to talk about what you deliver on?" I'd argue that you wouldn't be reading this book if you didn't feel that you had a career track record that is worthy of self-promoting.

> Follow your gut on the most strategic time to talk about your best practices and contributions. Simply by speaking openly about your results, what you can and cannot deliver, you demonstrate confidence and position yourself as a professional expert getting the airtime you deserve.

If you don't recognize your self-worth enough to talk openly about your value as a leader or even a powerful contributor to the process, then those thoughts are what others will pick up energetically and feel as well. People weigh in on how relevant you are based on how relevant you see yourself. You are rejecting yourself in advance before anyone else has the chance to every time you choose to fly under the radar. Who is responsible for broadcasting your achievements other than you? Those who buy into you are in reality buying into your results. Therefore, to be recognized for your achievements, you must start promoting them. The beauty of this process is that as you stand your ground and talk about what you have done well, you inevitably raise your confidence level, which energetically is what people will *instinctively* feel about you, as well as feel that they are in your trusted hands.

A frequent blind spot in the area of being one's own publicist becomes apparent when professionals seek to transition from being corporate leaders to working for themselves and starting a new business. They have a ton of experience working in various positions in the corporate structure, but when they turn to become entrepreneurs, they tend to throw away their big-ticket credibility factors as they struggle with a fraud factor—having difficulty in recognizing achievements as their own, and feeling that others would be better suited to successfully excel in their role. If you fall into this category, treat this as a white flag signaling that you need to surrender your limiting beliefs. Leverage your former experience and weave it into how you are an expert in your field. All your solid years of experience were not random. This is the backbone on which hangs your track record. Don't sideline it as a previous life you once had, swept under the rug.

You know what you know. Therefore, give yourself permission to speak about what you know—without worrying about all the aspects of your role that you may not have a full grasp of yet and can grow into. The divide between where you are and where you need to be is called the *growth gap*, and it signals where you can make the necessary investment in yourself so that others will invest in *you*.

COMPLIMENTS MARKET YOUR MISSION

Is your career goal to secure a better position with higher compensation or a new title that leverages you for the next career opportunity, or both? Although these goals may provide some true target areas, what motivates growth above all else is appreciation. If I could guarantee that each day your peers would express gratitude for your contributions, would you enjoy showing up at work, knowing that you are given that level of appreciation?

Successful leaders grow and build confidence by recognizing the value of their work not behind closed doors but by openly advocating for themselves, which, in turn, enables them to take on more challenging projects and roles. Recognition comes in many flavors. Often it comes in the form of compliments and positive feedback on past projects. Embracing this praise is embracing your value, which will inevitably lead to new opportunities because it locks in your belief in yourself, raising your confidence level and risk-taking tolerance.

If you look at any well-respected leaders, you'll find they are able to seek and accept bigger opportunities for advancement because of the very confidence they have garnered from a lifetime of smaller achievements. This is how you build confidence by starting small. By accepting recognition, you are not stroking your ego (although it should make you feel good about yourself); you are simply saying, "I deserve this appreciation. I deserve happiness and success." Then you own it. Looking at your career in this way, in small self-promotion increments, it becomes much easier over time for you to conquer your fear of how you will be perceived when selling yourself. You are trusting your instinct based on a string of informed decisions rooted in confidence and self-recognition.

> Care less about what people think and more about what you have to say and why you are qualified to say it.

Don't feel that you have a lifetime of achievements under your belt yet? Let's examine how well you receive praise, a fast-path tool for building confidence. When is the last time you authentically accepted a compliment related to your work without discomfort? As an educated professional and avid learner, you have likely received compliments throughout your career. Let's begin by recognizing them for what they are (and why you earned them) so that you can "unstick" your reaction to others, especially when they are direct beneficiaries of your work and your results. When you speak, glowing in your own light, rooted by what you know, make no mistake, others are listening. Your clients are listening not only to what you are saying, but to what you aren't saying as well; there is an unspoken understanding that you've considered their risks.

An underlying factor that can hold you back is an empathic mind-set that encourages you to think of yourself as a "mood sponge." This can cause you to be judgmental and hard on yourself. When you receive positive feedback or a high five from someone, keep in mind that you weren't just lucky. It wasn't one of your "good days." It also wasn't because of the fabulous team you had or the timing was just right. It was because of *you*. Can you see clearly when you have led a successful project or when your strategy was a key driver in reaching a shared goal?

Compliments are not meant to stroke the ego. They are strong instinctive pulses and motivators shown to improve higher achievement levels further. They are also a grateful gift. By not accepting them, you are, in reality, pushing away opportunities and suppressing your self-worth as a valuable service provider. You are essentially saying, "I'm not worthy of this gift." This attitude brings about circumstances where that underlying message overshadows your accomplishments not only in your career but also in other areas of your life, such as in your home, your finances, and your personal relationships.

Compliments stir loyalty. When suddenly someone offers to sing your praise to others and spread the word on the great job you've done, it's because you picked up the phone and made that phone call that allowed that person to get his or her project done, for example. In such situations, I encourage you to go beyond the obligatory "Thank you" and own the praise. Appreciate it, even if it takes days or weeks for you to receive it, which sometimes is the case. How you feel when you receive a compliment is very different from how you feel when you officially accept it. These are two varying-energy frequencies. There is no rule that you have to receive and accept a compliment at the same time. You can write it down or make a mental note so that you can come back to it later on. All compliments matter and contribute to your awareness of who you are at your core.

However you embrace a compliment professionally is likely the same way you treat a compliment personally. This is not just about your career; it's about the holistic you. Replaying a limiting belief will gain momentum quickly, and you'll suddenly find unwanted circumstances that reaffirm that negative thought repeatedly showing up. This holds you back until you are willing to turn the mental dial to allow more favorable thoughts in, recognizing your value. Accepting praise is what gives you credibility to speak anywhere and to anyone. When you look at it this way, you have quite a lot to share with others.

> *There is more hunger for love and appreciation*
> *in this world than for bread.*
> MOTHER TERESA

As an expert who delivers results, how do you embody *why* you do what you do so that others have no doubt about what you do brilliantly? Passion is what moves people. Emotion stirs loyalty. When you are aligned with your purpose, you can naturally deliver and advise others from that place of service, which is precisely when others begin to feel who you are and ultimately trust in your work. When dropping your name to refer you to others, people don't initially mention the work that you have done or the services you deliver. They share who you are first, then what you deliver. If years have gone by, often they may not even remember what you exactly do for a living, but they still trust that you are good at it because they enjoy being around you. Instinctively they remember how they *felt* when they were around you. This is what resonates with us as humans and what will keep you in line for new opportunities.

Meet Paula, a small-business owner in the pencil-making business. She has a small table set up at a school-sponsored event being held at an elementary school. A parent comes up to Paula and asks to buy some pencils for her daughter, who is in kindergarten. Paula sells her not only the pencils but also a pencil case, some multicolored scented erasers, and a pamphlet on proper penmanship for young children beginning to write. She then goes on to talk about how her pencils and products are fun, colorful, and motivating, proven to stimulate learning. This she has learned from the feedback she's received from parents in the local community.

Then Paula casually cites a funny story about a child who asked her for kiwi-flavored pencils. More parents stop by and hang around Paula's table for a while. They like her vibe. They feel good around her. Before they leave, they thank her and ask for a few of her business cards, which they can share with other parents whom they feel would love Paula's products.

A few weeks later, Paula receives a handwritten thank-you card from a parent. Her daughter loves using Paula's pencils when doing her homework. She goes on to praise her daughter for writing her name for the first time. Paula beams with pride, smiling on opening this grateful gift, and accepts these powerful words with an open heart. She goes on to talk about this glowing feedback with her family, friends, and clients.

Soon Paula begins to speak openly about why she entered the pencil-making business in the first place. For Paula, it wasn't really about pencils, although she loves making them. Her purpose is to make a difference for young children and have an impact on early childhood education. Everyone can feel Paula's why and what her values are.

When I was fairly green at navigating my way through the corporate workplace, if someone gave me a compliment on my hair, dress, or some deliverable I had churned out with my best-sweated effort, most times I felt awkward and pretty antsy, shooing away the godforsaken praise. It wasn't until I began speaking up about my best work, of which I was proud, that I understood how to receive praise well. Whether from me or from someone else, compliments began to make me feel good and raised my self-confidence.

If you're feeling awkward about receiving any kind of praise, you are falling into a limiting belief that you are not worthy of that gift.

It's as if someone pressed a little button inside you that produced the opposite of what you have been conditioned to believe, and therefore the praise would naturally feel like a lie. At your core, though, you know the truth—you deserve to be valued.

Self-esteem and praise are two common sources of parental feedback shown to shape young children's behavior.[1] Lack of positive feedback can account for why you hold onto that childhood admonition not to boast or celebrate yourself, or perhaps you received more criticism than praise. This hesitancy also could stem from years of being praised only for your physical features and not your intelligence.

Likewise, if you've convinced yourself that you don't deserve success, positive feedback on a job well done can feel like a one-time stroke of luck. "Watch out!" the ego screams. "You're setting yourself up for failure if you attempt to re-create that success again."

If you don't allow compliments to be bestowed upon you, then you are pushing good things away. When someone gives you a compliment, feel free to straighten up, look that person square on, and say, "Thank you," noticing how you feel.

> Self-promotion is your vehicle to keep doing what you love by talking about what you love so that everyone knows what you love to do brilliantly.

The four-letter *f*-word holding you back is *fear*, and it is at the heart of why you don't easily speak up about your accomplishments.

- Fear of failure
- Fear of rejection
- Fear of looking foolish
- Fear of being perceived as bragging

If you were to unpack this some more, you might find that there is also, on some level, fear of success. The fun part about fear, and the part that many people don't recognize, is that once you feel your fight, flight, or freeze response, you can then "out" the fear for what it is by openly sharing it with even one other person—there is strength in numbers. This instinctive awareness is how, for the most part, you dissipate your fear. Now you can push fear aside for the moment and focus on what you want to share. This is what deserves far more attention—your accomplishments through genuine self-promotion and recognition.

Rhonda is a successful business leader; yet she has had panic attacks for weeks, unable to sleep at the thought of being invited to speak on a stage at a large conference event as part of a panel of experts. When I asked Rhonda what her fear was, she said that she didn't know. She woke up in a heavy sweat imagining herself at the conference. We unpacked it some more together and discovered that it wasn't so much that Rhonda was afraid of speaking publicly. Her deepest fear was being asked a question that she didn't know the answer to. Holding her back was the fear of looking foolish. This fear showed up frequently in small meetings when she led presentations.

What could Rhonda say whenever this fear showed up? Here are some strong responses we came up with:

"That's a great question. Let me get back to you. I'll have to give more thought to that." [Acknowledge that you don't know, remaining genuine.]

"You know, I hadn't considered that. Great point! Here's what I do know." [Insert one expert opinion related to the question; then insert your expertise.]

[Ask the audience:] *"With a show of hands, how many people here also struggle with* [repeat the subject of the question]*?"* [Defer to the audience, engage, and include.]

"Great feedback. What's coming up from my gut is [insert an answer coming from intuition]. *Please connect with me*

after this event so that we can chat some more offline."
[Go with your gut response; follow up later.]

[Repeat the question. Buy some time to find a good response, and breathe. Your best answer is on its way.]

Don't you love it when you have options? Taking this approach, Rhonda aced that speaking opportunity and kicked her fear to the curb. Today I regularly see Rhonda genuinely self-promoting her expertise and extending her influence on LinkedIn, discussing her industry, sharing any valuable events she is about to attend, and recapping learning sessions she's had with her mentees, all tied together with her opinions. She regularly positions herself as a thought leader in her field and a person who shares resources with others to their benefit. Stepping into this kind of airtime was only possible once Rhonda (1) named the fear, (2) instinctively embraced being uncomfortable, and (3) ended her fear for good by chunking it down to simple actions she could take to respond to it.

SILENCE THE INNER CROW

I wish I can say that the inner crow eventually goes away, but, alas, there it is squawking in our ears every so often that we're not good enough to complete a new project, fill a new role, or grasp a new opportunity. New level, new devil! I've come to realize that this uninvited intrusion—the voice of limiting beliefs—is meant to keep us on our toes purposefully and with pencils sharpened.

I understand the inner crow all too well. As a corporate information technology (IT) leader who only knew how to speak geek in business discussing mainly technology, I recall how I walked this fraud factor rite of passage myself when I gave my first keynote on the topic of leadership. It was a subject I had never discussed on a public stage, and here I was addressing hundreds of people at a hotel in the heart of Manhattan. Until then, my sense of inclusion came only from those who wanted to hear me talk about technology, even though I had been coaching people in Financial Services behind closed doors for years. My ego held me in check: on paper, I was still a technologist.

Did I say what I needed to say that afternoon as a speaker, seeking to inspire people? I did, followed by a big round of applause. The audience, however, would never have guessed that my sweaty hands were clinging to the podium for dear life. I credit that blessed wooden crutch with preventing me from falling off the stage. It didn't matter to me that I had sweated it out the whole way. I had stepped into my biggest fear at the time. I had crossed over from technology guru to leadership expert in less than 60 minutes. There would never again come a time when I would not know how to speak publicly on a subject that I qualified myself to own and later influence.

When you break through your fear, you release it forever. This is much like brushing your teeth with your opposite hand for several days—your body will eventually adjust. The beauty of this process is that you will never go back to where you were. This then becomes your new normal: your body always knows the truth.

Not only does speaking to larger audiences fit into a powerful self-promotion strategy, but it also kicks in our need for love and acceptance. It's important to feel that we have what it takes to serve in this world and support others. This can't happen unless we accept ourselves first. Self-acceptance also shows up when you're sitting in an audience. It's the reason why you instinctively choose to sit in the front or the back of a room in any public venue. How visible do you want to be? How often do you wear bright colors as opposed to dark clothing? How well will you sell yourself if others aren't given a chance to meet and get to know you?

Love and acceptance rank right up there with the basic human need for food and shelter. When you are consistently churning the same limiting beliefs around in your mind, they become your reality and the very thing responsible for holding you back professionally. Those limiting beliefs control whether you pitch your ideas out loud or sweep them under the rug, allowing someone else's team to take the credit. It's the difference between picking up the phone and introducing yourself to someone who can help you and hiding behind your computer and hoping that someone sends you an email with a job prospect.

Your inner crow is subconscious and tends to kick in particularly when you're feeling tired or not eating well. Your ego is somewhat of a parasite in this regard, waiting in the wings for you to be at your most vulnerable when self-care is lacking. It's at your weakest point that you likely will replay stories in your head and talk yourself out of opportunities. It's why managing your energy level is so important to raising your confidence. The more grounded you feel, the more comfortable you are taking on more risk, whether that be speaking, asking the difficult questions, or making a key decision.

Look at your environment and the people you surround yourself with. Are you nurturing a suppressive mental state? If you can recognize how you're playing an equal role in this process, that's when you have the power to create change—when you are faced with making difficult decisions and are in the throes of discomfort. When you find yourself in this state, you must recognize that it is part of your growth path. This is when you realize that you don't have everything figured out but are willing to take one instinctive action despite the discomfort.

Let's assume that you and a peer are each given the same opportunity to advance to a new senior leader role. You each possess the same skill sets, education pedigree, and business experience and have been performing the same function for the same number of years. You are both offered the same increase in salary with the same number of direct reports on your new team. You cannot believe your luck. This is the very opportunity you have been seeking—only you assumed that it would happen one year from now. But *voilà!* It has landed at your feet! Your only next step is to say *yes* and make a move. You go home feeling enthusiastic about what the next few months will bring. You imagine the discussions you will lead, all the things you can bring to this role, and how you will make your new clients successful, all on your watch.

You also acknowledge that you were handpicked for this opportunity given your track record for achieving results.

Yet, in a slow and predictable turn of emotions, when you settle in at home that night, the self-sabotage thoughts kick in: "Am I good enough?" You attribute your past successes to your team rather than to your own achievements. The *impostor syndrome* shows up.

The impostor phenomenon was described by Pauline Clance and Suzanne Imes[2] as a psychological experience where one believes that one's accomplishments are not a result of one's true ability but instead are a result of having just been lucky or having worked harder than others and not able to be replicated again or, worse, a result of having manipulated other people into believing in your success. Right on cue, your inner crow can smell weakness in a heartbeat and begins to foster those dormant limiting beliefs. You do a mental self-assessment and realize you are only 60 percent qualified for this new leadership opportunity. You may need at least six months to a year to get yourself trained and gain enough experience to be entirely comfortable and hit the ground running. This thought further justifies and substantiates why you were planning on waiting one year to consider this career transition in the first place. Initially, your gut instinct leaped with joy at the prospect of a new opportunity. Later, your belief in yourself took a sharp U-turn. When you wait too long, instinct is replaced by reason.

You go into the office the next day and turn down the opportunity. Your colleague, in contrast, happily accepts the opportunity even though he or she also feels that 40 percent growth gap. The difference is that your colleague owns his or her authority swimmingly, while you remain stuck in the self-doubt spin cycle.

I can name dozens of circumstances where this story resurfaces. It happens when we feel others take credit for our work or feel undermined in meetings. In every case, if you are taking responsibility for your career, did you position yourself for advancement or quietly wait it out, hoping for the best until you were 100 percent ready? Did you follow your gut despite your fear of failure? Was leading a new team a consideration?

Reason replaces enthusiasm—that natural excitement that arises from taking on a challenging opportunity that has the potential to increase your influence. It's when you break this negative spin cycle that you achieve growth. It's when you look at that 40 percent growth gap, and instead of seeing it as something you lack, you see it as the breakthrough that will stretch and not freeze you. Now your 60 percent readiness can stretch a whole lot further than you initially thought.

Giving yourself the *yes* and self-qualifying to move forward suddenly become complicated when you put some skin in the game. Perhaps you need more time before you commit. This is the ego dance that plays in your mind if you allow it. See the ego as you would a small child who doesn't know that he or she has the potential to do flips and jumping jacks once that toddler takes the first step.

Good news—here are some promises that you can put your money on whenever you are banking on you:

- Will you thrive in a new role where you can double your influence but for which you are only 60 percent ready? *An absolute yes.*
- Will you feel uncomfortable for a while until you have mastered the business knowledge you need? *A highly confident yes.*
- Are the above two points reasons to stop you? *A no-nonsense no.*

Whatever the mind of man can conceive and believe,
it can achieve. Don't wait. The time will never be just right.
NAPOLEON HILL

The discomfort must be there because of the very nature of not knowing how you will accomplish your goal. The need to have the *how* all figured out is the perfectionist paralysis that has been holding you back. The only magic pill to get over a fear of failing is to leap right in. Consider that if the next opportunity didn't require you to sink your teeth in and grow, you wouldn't have sought it out in the first place.

It's when you feel out of your element taking on new responsibilities and challenges that you can make the most headway by riding out the storm and flexibly responding to change. You just roll up your sleeves and dive in with determination. This is also when you make the conscious decision to self-promote with ease and authenticity because you now have a strong sense of how to communicate the value you have added.

As a woman who inched her way up the corporate ladder for two decades, I know that it would be easy to say that the environment, the economy, internal politics, or even men were holding female leaders back from advancing into executive positions. However, this is not the reality I experienced. Yes, there were difficult circumstances that I could attribute to any one of those factors (and those barriers were not a figment of my imagination). What is also true is that when you focus on finger-pointing and blame, you give away your power and your ability to find a solution. Our choices and belief systems determine whether we thrive or just survive in that next venture. When you visualize your future success in a new opportunity, pay attention to what movie reel is playing in your mind. Are those images of you positive or negative? Are your instincts telling you that you're in a culture that would support your growth? If the answer is *no*, it's likely time to move on.

THE "NO-BRAGGING" BACKLASH

It's a reasonable discomfort—why would you opt to stick your neck out and high-five yourself openly in any given situation? Rather than squawking from a soapbox, you may prefer to hum with humility instead when you are asked to talk about your best work product. It's not the attention you seek. Still, there is an unspoken backlash to not singing your praises regularly. How you perceive yourself is the starting point for how others see you. If you are clear that your value is significant enough, including the results you get for people, then talking about those deliverables will guarantee that clients recognize those accomplishments too, so much so that they will undeniably be compelled to invest in you.

If, in contrast, you feel that you deserve only quiet mention, then that's about as much as people will remember about you as well. The risk of playing small with no self-promoting vein pumping throughout your body is that you will not be seen as memorable. This is no secret sauce. Speak up and often about what you do so that others also can rave about what you do. Inevitably, you will create opportunities for those people to want to work with you and hire you for the abilities you confidently project. This is your personal brand, defined by your raving fans.

If you're not singing from the rooftops about what you do, then you are pushing away the things that you want in your career. Energetically, you are telling all of those who are seeking your experience and skill sets and want to work with you that they don't need the results you deliver because you don't feel that they are relevant to mention.

How people perceive your value is directly related to how often you speak up about your value. Thus, self-promotion is a nonnegotiable communication strategy if you want to be a leader that people trust. Subconsciously, when you invest in something, you're also placing a weighted value on it. When you purchase a product, the conversation that's going on in your mind is: "What's the quality of this investment? Is it worth it? Will I get my money's worth?"

As a respected leader who readily self-promotes your best work, you're giving potential investors answers to those questions before they've had a chance to ask them. When you sign up for a free event that piques your interest, how likely will you attend without making a financial commitment? The probability of your participating is far higher when you make the investment and pay for it up front. In other words, you perceive the benefit of something only when you attach a value to it and put some skin in the game. This same mindset applies to self-promotion. People will happily tune in to what you have to offer, giving you their time and making the investment, when they perceive your value. With that said, who, then, is responsible for showcasing your product value other than you?

In terms of career and life, how have you invested in yourself with professional and personal development? Breakthroughs don't happen when you feel comfortable and safe. Transformation begins when you make a commitment to yourself and are willing to be held accountable to your goals, whether seeking a new job, relationship, or home. People will invest in you as much as you invest in yourself.

YOUR NO-ACTION ACTIONS

It is not only what we do, but also what we do not do,
for which we are accountable.
MOLIÈRE

If you don't feel ready to make bold moves in your career, have you asked yourself what the risk is of staying where you are? A pattern I've noticed over the last 20 years of coaching professionals is that as humans, we can easily disregard the fact that when we take no action, we are still taking action. We choose to do nothing. Yet isn't that the language the people on your future leadership team want you to speak? They want to hear you talk about the results and benefits, but they also expect you to voice the risks. What is going to happen if they don't go in a particular direction? "Is there a real opportunity lost if we don't spend X amount of budget dollars on this and use the money elsewhere?" Your no-action actions are a very tangible thing to keep in mind when you are communicating in business, especially when your instinct is nudging you to move on. No action *is* action when you choose to stay silent and is as tangible as speaking up.

If knowledge is power, then implementation is influence. What are the no-action actions that are working against you in your life? These are the things that you are not doing, and they are hurting your chances of opportunities and conversations that you should be having right now. I'm speaking about the situations where you have been silent, when you did not chime in with an idea, agree to disagree with someone, make that phone call, leverage a unique opportunity and instead accepted that you are not getting that promised promotion even though your team outperformed every initiative under your leadership. All these no-action actions are what you chose despite your gut instinct nudging you otherwise. Each time you silence your inner dialogue, you're making a choice. You are choosing to do nothing, which can later turn out to look like something very different and unwelcome from what you've imagined. You're choosing to say, "My words don't matter, so I'll remain small and silent." This offers people no insight into your value and what you can potentially bring to an opportunity. This is not a judgment call; it's a flag to becoming aware of when you may be quietly opting out. To create change, you first need clarity on what needs to be changed.

It's easy to fall prey to lying low, waiting things out, and hoping that everything turns out for the best. A word of warning: doing nothing produces nothing. No action equates to no results. How does sitting on your hands feel versus taking small action steps that nudge you out of your comfort zone toward something that you really want?

Here's where taking no action shows up in our lives each time every time:

No-action action: You don't recognize your past successes as being worthy of speaking about openly.

Backlash: You are compensated accordingly. No exciting projects or clients come down the pipeline. Hence, no income increase or bonuses are given for initiatives you led or participated in.

No-action action: You don't share the impact of your team's projects and instead focus on typical operational activities.

Backlash:	You are perceived as someone who excels at keeping the lights on but not a leader who can institute change.
No-action action:	You hold back your objecting opinion on a project's approach.
Backlash:	You forgo your right to speak up later on and complain about it. You have weakened your position by remaining silent. No one respects the person who quietly sits on the sidelines and yet is quick to place blame and judgment with an "I told you so" later on.

How you handle challenging circumstances in one area of your life likely indicates how you deal with them in all areas. Don't fall prey to thinking, "If I just wait another year for the next opportunity, I will be ready." There's a price tag to taking that "wait-and-see" approach. When you're not putting out feelers that you are well qualified and confidently ready to take the leap of faith banking on you, leveraging what you know, then the world responds accordingly. Your desires fall on deaf ears, and you run the risk of remaining stuck where you are.

What does your instinct tell you when you continue to tolerate an environment that ignores positive performance and promotes unprofessionalism and a lack of courtesy? What would be the next best action you can take right now when there is an evident lack of leadership and vision in your organization? How will you be successful in one year if the directives are always changing from your leaders? What does the picture look like one year from today if you stay where you are?

There are risks and costs to action.
But they are far less than the long-range
risks of comfortable inaction.
JOHN F. KENNEDY

What no-action actions have you been taking? There is no shame or blame if you have tolerated a culture in which there are no opportunities for growth. No regrets! Perhaps you trusted what was promised to you in terms of advancement or found a comfortable work-life balance. It was a trade-off you were willing to make because it had a clear payoff. Raising a family or taking care of a sick relative, for example, may have been your priority at the time. Today, however, your needs have changed. What's the next best move you can make that showcases your expert value and can be more impactful in terms of appreciation for your value? What's the risk if you do nothing? Consider all areas of your life: health, finances, family, home. There's always a choice.

Globally, companies understand the cost of taking no-action actions and will not hesitate to respond to public criticism that calls for leaders to step down from positions of authority after being accused of racism or gender bias. No action in this case is being perceived as an endorsement of unacceptable behavior. Swift action is broadcasting public statements that solidify a position of zero tolerance toward discrimination and harassment. This is also why diversity and inclusion programs are moving to the forefront of company mission statements and board agendas.

> **Leader.** Noun; a person who leads or commands a group, organization, or country. Leaders take the initiative in an action and are examples for others to follow.

If you have valuable experience and knowledge, then release the dam and unleash your expertise. If you have expertly led a successful business function over time, then somewhere down the road you have found creative solutions to problems. You may not be getting recognition for those solutions today because you are not speaking openly about them. Without any airtime, you run the risk of being pigeonholed as the well-liked professional who may get the job done but also as someone who enjoys flying under the radar, perceived as having no desired influence to champion change. The same theme is at play when you do not accept compliments, shooting down the likelihood of others advocating for you through referrals.

You have a purpose. It's the reason you chose your current vocation and what drives those you serve. Once you say *yes* to that purpose, by accepting compliments, owning your strengths, and recognizing your worth, you garner your energy, and attract the people, resources, and opportunities you need to reach your goals. Without purpose as your compass, goals and action plans are meaningless.

Without openly speaking of your results, you never give people the opportunity to "size you up," let alone determine whether you are someone they can trust. When you speak with pride and passion about a project that went well on your watch and freely admit the mistakes you learned from in that experience, in contrast, others will feel your confidence and vulnerability. They will see themselves in you. Through your example and leadership, you've just given them permission to call themselves out and be somewhat vulnerable as well. Keep in mind that not everyone may agree with you, but they will respect you, and your expert opinion will still resonate for them on its own.

People can feel that you care and that your heart is in your work. As a leader, your job is to reassure your clients that you have their best interests in mind and always remain a few steps ahead of them to keep them out of trouble. In contrast, without trust in place, you run the risk of being perceived as someone who is aloof to the blind spots, without a strategy, and who doesn't deliver meaningful value.

Consider a situation in which you have an uneasy feeling working with a peer. The person appears to have no pulse on what is going on, even within his or her own team and projects. Admittedly, the person may have been there in body, but mentally, wasn't he or she always perceived as being checked out? Such people appear to walk around with blinders on, perfectly satisfied with their little corner of the world, and shut down from anything that is outside their responsibility, protecting their territory. You know what it's like to work with professionals cut from this "not-on-my-watch" cloth. You also know that they are not sought after and offer little in the way of insights or recommendations.

Leading During a Crisis

It's not uncommon to find yourself in an organization that is struggling and in crisis one day, whether financially, from sudden acquisitions, or as a result of structural changes. How you handle and survive any kind of crisis is a true test of leadership. It would be easy to see your organization doing what many others do to save themselves and stay afloat. Cut the people first to save top-down costs, and expect those still remaining to roll up their sleeves and work twice as hard. Making a mindset shift, however, this isn't a problem; rather, this is an intuitive nudge for you to ask the following question: "How can I turn this circumstance into an opportunity on my terms?"

When you're able to step to the side, outside yourself, and see a situation not as happening *to* you but as a third-party observer, you instinctively will know what to do when, for a moment, you take responsibility for that difficult circumstance. When you can turn this around, assuming you are responsible, what would you do differently? This process is the basis of creative thinking—the ability to be open-minded and address problems from a fresh perspective and new vantage point. This gives you the opportunity to find a different set of results and a new solution.

Taking responsibility for your career is recognizing that it's your job, no one else's, to crawl yourself out of the troubling situation and ask from your gut, "What is it that I can learn here? How am I being called to step up and grow?" If you're not sure that you are in an environment that supports your growth, ask yourself these questions:

"One year from today, where will I be?"

"Will I have learned and grown enough to be better off than I am now?"

"Will I remain at the status quo in leadership, or will I have lost precious time?"

In other words, what's the risk if you choose to stay, or is it time for you to move on? If instinctually you're ready to leave, how will you protect your team before you exit?

Systematize Your Success

Start with the scars (without reliving them). Opening up past wounds only to look back and figure out what went wrong will not serve you well. However, when you go back to times when you felt defeated and came out shining on the other end, you chose decisive action to address unfavorable circumstances. Take note of all these life learning experiences and recognize how you made it through so that you can do it again when new challenges swing back around and you are being called on to provide more leadership.

This is called *systematizing your success* and is a cornerstone of promoting what you're selling—yourself. Looking back, you can determine what worked well in your career, what didn't work at all, and what you can do better. Turn to the people, projects, and environments where you felt knocked down at every turn, trying to churn out the best results for your clients. Despite those circumstances, you didn't just survive; you thrived! You found authentic ways to navigate difficult personalities and likely challenging politics, you discovered creative solutions that got the job done, and you found new ways to solve old problems, instituting change.

> *People don't invest in you so much as*
> *they are investing in what you can do for them.*

As a technology leader, I often had to put my ego in check—after all, we weren't curing cancer. When there was a work crisis where some technical process went rogue, my management would refer to our mission as one that must "stop the bleeding." This was a call to action to get a problem fixed fast. After we addressed a crisis successfully, I'd find the ideal time at meetings, based on instinct, to talk about the picture before the bloodshed and the heroism of my team during our rescue mission. These were excellent prime-time venues to instinctually share our expertise and self-create platforms to inject subtle storytelling about the obstacles we faced and overcame. We spotlighted why we could be trusted should the lights ever turn off again. Self-promoting, storytelling, speaking from a place of passionate pride, addressing your fumbles, and showcasing the ways your team thrived through collabo- ration are all part of your leadership strategy to demonstrate your value with authenticity and ease.

LEVERAGE YOUR LEADERSHIP ASSETS

Have you traditionally been the leader who enjoys sinking your teeth into one business area and continually deep diving from there through- out your career? If not, then perhaps you are someone who prefers to go wide instead, spanning several subject matter areas but not necessarily being considered an expert in any.

Deep dive or wide approach, there's no right or wrong answer. Both career paths serve you. The latter typically sets you up for more leadership, having the exposure and solid understanding of various functional shops across the organization. The former can be a balance between domain leadership and expertise in which you opt to remain somewhat hands-on, for example by leading day-to-day operations and occasionally learning a new skill when needed to keep a project mov- ing. Be clear on the leadership asset category you occupy so that you can speak to and "sell" the knowledge you have earned.

You can promote other leadership assets, such as your experience in past roles and the products and services you developed along the way. You can speak to the workflows and processes and how they best serve your clients and why. You can segue into highlighting yourself as the resource to whom most people turned to accomplish their goals, even if you excelled at delegating to find help in those engagements. You were still relied on to find the right person to solve the problem.

Your experience navigating "the system," knowing how things get done in an organization and how to lead through change and return positive results, is what you are qualified to openly self-promote. Your understanding of the end-to-end flows that move across departments, "bridging the gap" when communication breaks down, is a topic you can (and should) bring to the forefront, highlighting your value.

Where do you rank on the wisdom scale in your field? Don't fall prey to self-sabotage, thinking that you don't have any insights. If you simply have a steady finger on the pulse of how business moves in your industry, that counts. If you have come to your own conclusions about trends, you are an expert authority. Therefore, your opinions on these trends hold value and are prime-time assets to socialize.

Let's look at other leadership assets. How have you led others with your expert value? Consider when you were once thrown into a new project as its champion because no one else was available or stepped up. What does that "take-charge" backstory look like, and how did that situation play out? There were likely many times when you were not officially in a leadership role but stepped in anyway to ensure the work was completed, there again demonstrating your leadership value.

- Have you taken on someone else's responsibilities when the person was out because of parental or disability leave, for example?
- Have you mentored someone in your career? This could have been in the form of training, where you walked someone through best practices.
- Was there any technical or functional skill that you became so well known for that coworkers kept knocking on your door seeking help to do their jobs better?

It's not only what you've done on paper that you can promote. Think about the experience and skills you have gained from all the responsibilities you owned as a natural impulse over the years. They paint a telling picture of who you are and how you have led.

Seeking new technologies and ways of working more efficiently are what drew me to a tech career. I'd embrace new software that crossed my desk, seeking to learn if it could support my team and our clients better. I'd often pick up the phone and call our suppliers, letting them know the pros and cons of what our experience was while allowing them to perfect it further in their next rollout. Surprisingly, this outreach led to speaking opportunities. Suppliers became business partners who would take me out to lunch, followed by personal invitations to represent their products to their clients, hence promoting *their* value at conferences. I took this offer every time, recognizing the social proof these suppliers gained from building their brands behind these gestures. As an offshoot, having my name listed as a speaker on the lineup at IT conferences enabled me to leverage my influence with large audiences and further get my name out there.

These newly formed speaking chops gave me the exposure I needed to hear about unpublished job opportunities. People in the crowd would greet me off stage with a firm, open handshake and later happily refer me on after the traditional business card swap. Had I not allowed myself to be uncomfortable, to follow my instinct by pursuing new ways to communicate, those opportunities would have never presented themselves.

Pursuing activities that you enjoy not only brings passion to your work, which makes you feel accomplished, but also radiates positive energy that others will *feel*. You can cherry-pick opportunities to market yourself at any given time, whether you are standing on line to pay for a coffee or joining a 5K walkathon with peers.

Your low-hanging fruit lies within the grasp of those who have expressed interest in learning more about what you do. These are the people whom you want to stay in touch with because they can refer you on to their management or other decision makers. Keep a list of these contacts close, and don't lose it. They have given you permission to knock on their doors and nudge them later on, without ever needing to feel awkward about it.

If you were to ask various business leaders what the top desired skills are that they look for in their hires, financial and business acumen are *not* at the top. Guess what tops their wish list? They are looking for leadership gusto, excellent communication skills, and a personal charm factor that sells.

Whether you recognize it or not, your charisma and natural way of being—your *soft skills*—are what attracts people to you. If you are witty or have a wicked sense of humor, bring it to any and all conversations. People who spend half their lives at work want to hang out with people who are pleasant to be around. You may have a successful career track record that speaks volumes, or your education and skill sets may have opened the door for you to walk into the room; but make no mistake—it's your personality and charm that keep you seated at the table. People can perceive immediately that you are someone who will fit in with their culture, which holds no small amount of weight when you consider organizations that place their employees, team building, and collaboration at the top of their inclusion agenda.

Your soft skills work like a charm because they stir loyalty and build trust and influence over time. These are the qualities that make a great leader and that motivate people and teams to execute on your vision. The best way to showcase your soft skills is to simply be a good storyteller.

Soft Skills and Storytelling

> *Marketing is no longer about the stuff that you make,*
> *but about the stories you tell.*
> SETH GODIN

Admittedly, what I always look for when I interview someone is whether I could picture myself working with that person daily. Will he or she step up when duty calls and take charge, or will I have to spoon-feed him or her? Can the person be led and also lead others?

Your personality is one that people will naturally gravitate to when you can answer the above questions. Are people's like-minded energy felt in the organization's DNA? This also goes both ways. You can walk into a culture and immediately sense dysfunction and a top-down leadership style that leaves nothing to the imagination when it comes to how the leaders do business and treat their employees. Listen to your instincts, especially when entering new environments.

Owning your unique value and then self-promoting it must be authentically aligned with your personality. This is a self-actualizing journey that begins with mastering your mental game, embracing your beliefs about your talents, and remembering that success is your own definition. When you're clear on what you deliver *and* can also communicate those results naturally through your unique personality, that's when you are paid what you're worth.

Now you might be confident in having strong expertise in your field, maybe there's no doubt in your mind, but that doesn't necessarily mean that you're always selling it effectively. In contrast, you might be self-promoting regularly, but that doesn't mean that you're communicating it well enough that in your clients' view, they trust you, and you're hitting their pain points.

The world does not pay you for what you know as much as it pays you for what you can deliver. What results do you promise? Keep in mind that you can't commit to promises if you haven't taken the time to understand your client's challenges. Instinctively, this is why you know that you are qualified to lead them. Subconsciously, everyone wants to be led. Your managers want you to lead them. Your clients want you to lead them. Your prospects (those not yet trusting you) want you to lead them. They want to sleep well at night knowing that you have their backs.

So how are you going to sell it? It is so easy to fall short in recognizing your strengths because you've been in it for so long. This is about being your own publicist and also being clear on your results, which can easily get swept under the rug. Yet you are the driver to people hiring you and keeping you in mind for new opportunities.

In a climate of leading remote teams, communication prevails. You're going to need to motivate and amplify results beyond email and video-based meetings. This is the intersection of your personality, expertise, and results that allows you to toot your own horn with authenticity and ease, even if you consider yourself somewhere on the introverted spectrum.

If past performance predicts future success, then success leaves clues. People who put their faith in your leadership are looking for you first to paint the picture of what you can bring to that next role or project. In other words, how can you benefit them? A storytelling strategy that conveys your value is to speak to your future impact. Although past achievements matter, it's just as important to talk about the results you have yet to bring to a role, as if you have already been given that opportunity.

An intriguing difference found between men and women is that when it comes to self-promotion, women tend to talk about what they achieved (past tense). Yet a carefully tuned ear will hear men speaking to the future consistently. Men are perceived as having no qualms about self-promoting all the projects they will (future tense) slam-dunk in a few short sentences. Even the most reserved men advocate for themselves, steadily squeeze in airtime whenever they can, to sell their value and secure their seniority.

To showcase your authentic self, when you lead from your gut, rest assured that you can navigate any discussion because you will tap into how you feel. This is when you instinctively share a random story because it feels right. You can talk about challenges you have dealt with in the past, painting the before and after pictures you experienced. You can talk about where you would hope to see a role, project, or function evolving in six months—drawing out your vision but, more relevant, demonstrating your beliefs in that vision. This is a confidence that is felt all around. You can talk about the weekend and what you did with your children or dog. This is no secret sauce. Soft skills establish and set the tone for who you are. They elicit unscripted storytelling, where you instinctively share a narrative that feels right in a given conversation and then let it go. Your stories have the power to inspire and demonstrate how you want to be perceived.

You will know you are doing a good job of advocating for yourself and sharing personal stories when you can turn into a self-promotion chameleon. This is where you can change your colors and communicate in any environment and conversation, speaking to those who couldn't be more different from you. They can have green hair and tattoos up and down their arms, but you still give them the results they're looking for. When you can walk into a conversation naturally and project confidence in your ideas, with a commitment to results, that's when you know that you are self-promoting effectively. Instinctively, you will feel it—through no rhyme or reason, you just know.

COMMUNICATE YOUR METRICS

If you subscribe to the belief that setting goals is essential to your career, then if you were to fast-forward six months from now, how would you measure success? When you are speaking of your value, share it in terms of metrics. Now, you might say, "My track record speaks for itself. I've always met my targets and have built a reputation for my team being dependable and delivering on time every time."

That's great, but that's not enough if you can't quantify those successes and socialize them. Measuring your success is no more than taking all the things you have achieved and wrapping some metrics around them. In an authentic self-promoting vein, metrics are a key indicator of success, and success must be quantifiable.

Here's why showcasing your personal metrics matters in your career:

1. Those who hire you want the short and sweet version of your accomplishments so that you can go on and continue that proven track record for them.
2. You become a magnet for opportunities, gaining more influence when you can speak in terms of your scorecards. Your managers also speak in terms of scorecards, and

therefore their success is directly tied to how well you
perform.

3. You can focus on critical areas to measure your impact,
which, in turn, drives your confidence and how effectively
you communicate your influence when presenting to a wider
audience.

Here's how it works: whatever information you share in narrative
form, you now speak in terms of time, units, dollars, and percentages.
Your clients want to hear the savings achieved, the costs cut, and the
efficiencies implemented and would appreciate it if you dropped the
long-winded version behind all the data. They want you to neatly package it all up and give it to them in small chunks that are easy to digest and
remember. Metrics satisfy a desire for people to be able to "sum you up."

Let's look at the leadership metrics of a leader in the medical field.
His or her numbers would be based on how many patients, on aver-
age, he or she saw each week or the number of surgeries performed in
a month. If the leader works on the research side, the numbers could
reflect how many research papers he or she has published, the number
of fellowships granted, how many trainees the leader had, or the per-
centage of patient waiting time reduced in the leader's practice.

Instinctively, your audience knows at this moment what metrics
sum you up. When communicating your value in terms of metrics, use
the following strategy, which others can retain long after your meeting or discussion ends: cut down whatever you were planning to say,
summarizing a weekly status report, for example, and throw out a metric instead. Here are some examples of how to highlight your value
succinctly:

> "We achieved 85 percent savings *by replacing the legacy paper
> approval process with an automated electronic expense system,
> saving our team* more than 10 hours a month."

> "We streamlined the time it takes to get a client onboarded from
> four days to one."

"We have cut down a patient's waiting time from 40 *to* 15 *minutes, increasing the number of patients seen by* 20 *percent every week."*

This is your measurable track record. Metrics make your work not only more memorable, but more important, and they also show deep respect for others' time by getting to the point and keeping it simple. Considering your next career move, what metrics would you need to own and self-promote to get there? What metrics effectively market your message?

A simple example of speaking your numbers is sharing a graphic that represents all the background information and volumes of data you have gathered and rolled up for others, thereby helping them connect the dots. Whether the graph comes from a spreadsheet or your own analysis, an opinion can be easily formed from looking at the data. Marketing teams focused on growth excel at depicting their results because they're easy to illustrate and measure. They can easily create a snazzy graph that charts a campaign, simply showcasing the number of leads in the pipeline and client conversions.

A leader is a marketer who can sell his or her brand.

Those who hang out on the business networking hub LinkedIn will immediately note your measure of influence when your profile has reached more than the 500-person threshold of connections. Here again, you are sized up by a key performance indicator: How many people are tuning in to you and want to hear what you have to say?

Let's take the same formula and apply it to any business site you visit for the first time. The number of testimonials and how diverse the consumers are will play a role in whether you ultimately make a purchase. The photos and videos tell a story of how inviting and approachable the company is.

If you're a writer, you may also market yourself through the written word—how many articles you have published demonstrates your level of influence. Successful marketing campaigns will use the following metrics to drive how well their product's message lands. The top motivators that make consumers want to buy make the following statements:

"Here's how much money we will help you make: . . ."

"Here's how much money we will help you save: . . ."

"Here's how much time we will help you protect: . . ."

"Here's how much effort we will help you eliminate: . . ."

Likewise, when you speak your own metrics, your clients want to hear the savings you have made, the costs you have cut, and the efficiencies you have implemented. These are your measurable benefits. Your clients also rely on you to share the measurable costs. If your team chooses to divert its time and spend it elsewhere, your clients want to hear the impact this decision has on delaying a critical project, such as the number of days their projects will potentially fall behind. Metrics are used as key indicators of the potential for success or failure of your client's projects, speaking to the benefits and risks. People will always appreciate when you drop the long version of the story behind your data research and present your proposals so that they are easy to digest and remember.

In everyday advertisements, we see examples of odd number metrics for which so far there is no psychological explanation but that still make for extremely effective sales campaigns. For example:

"Five ways martial arts will help your child raise his or her confidence and grades in school—join now!"

"Three sweat-free under-15-minute workouts that you can do in your living room—get started now!"

"Seven inexpensive makeup tips to hide skin discolorations on your face—buy now!"

Here's what your marketing campaign should sound like:

"The new approach we used to trend product profitability showed a 15 percent increase in revenue than previously expected."

"Employee turnover has dropped 60 percent in the last two years because of the compensation incentives, flex-time, and training opportunities we made available at all levels."

Any metric you decide on is a good one if it showcases the value you deliver. The most critical metric, however, which you want to use to measure yourself against consistently for your entire career and life, is *how often you speak up.* Speaking up is the number one predictor of your success.

This applies to any area of your life—whether you are managing your finances, buying a new car, negotiating a home purchase, finding a life partner, or discussing feedback with your child's teacher; speaking up is the number one top predictor of your success. If you take yourself seriously as a business leader who has value, then it's your responsibility to speak to your beliefs, speak to your results, speak to your experience, speak to your challenges, speak to your failures, and speak to your ideas.

It is your responsibility to *speak up.*

In a 20-year study of students from Stanford Business School, Professors Bradley Hanson and Thomas Harrell looked for what they called the "success factor"—the number one identifiable predictor of success. What they came up with was something they called "social extroversion," or the ability to speak up. This seems like such a simple thing, but it was present in every successful person and absent in those for whom life was a struggle.[3]

The more often you speak up—to any size audience, whether one person or one hundred—the higher are your chances of success. You can make it a daily gutsy trigger before you go to bed. Ask yourself, "On a scale of 1 to 10, how well did I speak up today?" If the answer is hovering somewhere between 1 and 5, you're probably not advocating for yourself enough.

It's easy to get caught up in how people perceive us, whether we belong in conversations or meetings, or whether we have anything valuable to add. This then becomes a self-fulfilling prophecy. As long as you hold onto this limiting belief, you cannot market yourself, let alone your results. The next time someone asks, "So what is it that you do?" before you respond with the textbook answer, be clear on your response to the more relevant question first: "How do I want to be perceived?"

Professionals who have demonstrated leadership but tend to be quiet and humble admittedly share that they have often felt misunderstood. They are either treated as pushovers or perceived as disinterested in their work because they don't speak up enough and voice their opinions. This is often seen when someone is just starting in a new role, where the natural tendency is to scope things out and observe the environment before sticking one's neck out too far and piping in at meetings.

In the work I have done with female surgeons and women in medical research, it has become apparent that their humility has often led to their own professional demise (when they did not voice their opinions as leaders in their field).

First impressions matter. A first perception that shows you to be a backseat driver can become "sticky." Instinctively, when you feel this happening (which energetically you must if you're "people-reading" how you are being perceived), flip this safe and comfortable approach around and be more vocal in one-on-one and group discussions. Ask powerful questions. Although you can't predict how people will react to you, you can control your image and manage that perception.

Reflecting on the early years of my career, I recognize where I had appeared more she-woman strong because I had a lot more to prove at the time. This substantiated for me how perception means everything and how cultures naturally develop. Keep in mind that your team and clients will only go as far as you give yourself permission to learn and grow; back then, when I was a lot younger, admittedly, I took myself too seriously.

We saw a true example of the power of perception when American tennis player Serena Williams openly disputed with an umpire who accused her of cheating and called a violation at the US Open. Seething, she threw her racket down and called him a "liar" and a "thief." In the global arena of public opinion, her dramatic pushback was judged to be an overreaction. On the other hand, many felt if it were a male tennis player who exhibited the same actions, the behavior would be considered a passionate response instead of a negative display of overemotion. The circumstance demonstrated how men and women are perceived differently when they speak boldly. Being assertive and clearly communicating with intention, using your authentic personality is more meaningful than molding your behavior to match expectation based on gender.

If you're willing to play full on in all areas of your life with authenticity, do you tend to throw down your chips and be who you are when there's nothing left to lose or hold yourself back when everything's at stake? It's not so easy to speak up when there's more at risk and why it's considered a gutsy move. When you trust your instincts, you raise your confidence, which empowers you to increase your risk tolerance over time and further grow in *self-leadership.*

When you make the commitment to self-promote, do it with full spirit so that you are sharing not only what you do brilliantly as a professional expert but, more importantly, who you are. Talk candidly about your accomplishments with pride and enthusiasm, and then wrap some telling metrics around them so that you remain memorable.

Your experience and reputation stand on their own. You'll become desensitized to what people think of you because of that solid self-image you've established. You'll sell your value through service—sharing your skills, education, and intuitive know-how.

Successful leaders have years of making split-second decisions when under intense pressure. However, their overall success rate from making those gut instinct decisions didn't develop on day one. They have years of experience and any number of unpredictable failures under their belts. They can't rationalize their perspective or explain it; they simply trust how they feel. They look at the facts in their files or all the shaking heads at the table disagreeing with the direction they propose, and they will act anyway despite that feedback. Trusting their instinct, they can provide no scientific explanation—they just *know*.

You don't need to sell this strength; you begin to make strong decisions through increased trust in your instincts and in yourself. You become confident by thinking on your feet, showing the lessons you learned, and learning to trust your instinct based on those experiences. A positive offshoot of this approach is that you also become desensitized to pressure over time; it naturally becomes of use much like any muscle in your body that kicks in when needed. Your path becomes clear when your intuition becomes your best strength and decision-making tool.

Following your instincts is learning to trust yourself and thus the decisions you make. As a result, you are empowered to trust in others—the ability to let go and let others "run with it" versus handling (but perceived to be controlling) activities on your own. Like it or not, we all have a perception to manage. Some executives share that they have noticed a pattern when stepping into a new role: they tend to rub people the wrong way up front, including their new team. However, later, after some time has passed, usually around the six-month mark, they freely let down their guard and only then build trust. This cautious behavior could likely show up outside of a career as well, such as in personal friendships and family relationships.

Anything you do is everything you do. As a leader in any area of your life, how do you trust, and how do others develop trust in you?

OWN YOUR
AUTHORITY AS A
THOUGHT LEADER
WITH INFLUENCE

If your actions inspire others to dream more,
learn more, do more, and become more, you are a leader.
JOHN QUINCY ADAMS

EXPERTS ARE MADE, NOT BORN

Some professionals get turned off by the pretentious tone that the term *thought leadership* evokes, unsure whether it is a characteristic they can call their own. It is an earned attribute and popular buzzword that highlights business leaders who are relied upon as credible authorities in their industries and who can influence action. Such leaders leverage their experience, skill sets, lessons learned, intuitive insights, and compassion by packaging their mastery of a subject matter for others to digest and on which to base their decisions. My goal is to hold up the mirror and help you understand why you should consider yourself a thought leader as well.

There's a certain growth path that you take after being in your chosen vocation over time. The root word of vocation is *vocare*, which means "being called to something" and "being purpose driven." Reflecting back to when you just started out in your career, at some point you had to learn the ropes in that new role. Over time, you enjoyed doing your job so well that you eventually forgot that it takes rudimentary steps one, two, and three to accomplish it. Eventually, you mastered it so gracefully that you could do it in your sleep, until one day, you simply stopped and said to yourself, "Hang on a minute. I am churning out my best work, doing a brilliant job. Do I want to remain here forever? I have the potential to take on more leadership with more compensation and gain more growth opportunities. I have a rock-solid career record I can lean on. I want more. I deserve more. I am more."

Consider this your instinctual "aha moment" of self-qualifying as a thought leader in your field. This is where we fall short when we compare ourselves with those we consider to be influencers. We assume that "making it" in our careers is getting the corner office (which does not exist anymore given the open floor plans of our digital age), earning the weighty title, and being hailed for our years of service at company-wide events.

Opening the kimono, however, thought leadership is simply self-awareness, knowing that you can serve your constituents in a bigger way as an advisor with a portfolio of best practices and proven results. It's answering the call, no longer waiting to be called. It takes guts to allow yourself to see your bigger reflection in the mirror.

As a thought leader, you can pull essential information from various bushels of knowledge and package it into a bountiful basket of coherent standards, ideas, solutions, insights, and recommendations for those who are eager to learn from, act on, and ultimately benefit from. True thought leaders surround themselves with a team that becomes even better at its own role because their members have done their jobs so well. This is the moment in your career when you get paid for how you think and advise, going broader as an expert authority in your field.

Your results speak for themselves, based on those *quantifiable* metrics discussed in Chapter 1 and cultivating your brand from self-promotion. Here you are expanding your leadership scorecard, leveraging your soft metrics—those that make up your *qualitative* yardstick, that cannot easily be summed up on paper yet are impactful because you visibly remain in service and are providing value, informing and motivating others.

These soft metrics are demonstrated when others can depend on you to, for example, keep a pulse on the market trends, communicate the risks, break down the silos across departments, bridge teams together, and keep an eye out for compliance flags, legal and regulatory changes, and the likelihood that the organization could be affected by all those factors and more. These skills also kick in when it's clear that your job is to have your clients' backs; you are their eyes and ears and understand their market, swooping down, in "helicopter" mode, where needed in the final hour and keeping them and their organizations safe from harm. Being competent in identifying themes and trends happening at your organization and in the wider industry at large supports your ability to pitch your bigger vision and think strategically to connect those themes and trends to bottom-line results.

No human who strives for growth and starts out on a given path (personal or professional) remains satisfied being on that path forever. You will always want to take on more and keep an eye out for the next best thing in your life. The world is continuously expanding, and so must you. Placing a thought leader title on your career profile, granted, would appear egotistical. Recognizing that you are a leading expert in a given subject area, however, is "owning" your authority. This is becoming clear about where you are and, more importantly, where you want to be in your career as someone who can offer a unique perspective to others. This is not to say where you are right now is stunting your advancement and holding you back. Every position is a stepping-stone and opportunity for you to move into more leadership and increase your influence. In fact, whenever you start in any new role, on day one, you are always looking ahead to where you will be in one year's time. In other words, ask yourself, "What would have to happen for me to be successful a year from now?" If you were a fly on the wall, what must you see to measure your accomplishments? Knowing your qualitative metrics helps you gain clarity on what to focus on, which clients to give the most attention to, and how to navigate a political landscape that strengthens your instinctual radar when it comes to making the best decisions to support your efforts.

> *Wisdom is not a product of schooling*
> *but of the lifelong attempt to acquire it.*
> ALBERT EINSTEIN

Your Growth: How Much and By When?

Having more leadership and influence can take many different forms. It can mean having more people to lead, running an enterprise-wide project, being sought after as a speaker or advisor, or even picking one spot in a functional area and taking on more responsibility. It can also mean sitting on a board of directors.

Success is based on what you define as growth right now. It's the answer to "How much leadership do I want? When do I want to get there?" Instinctually, you can always feel when you're being nudged toward a new growth stage. Yet here's the rub: it usually comes with discomfort from those previously mentioned three fears: rejection, failure, and looking foolish.

Whether you are a project manager, a trainer, an accountant, an analyst, or a sales manager—any role you fill—if you believe that you have delivered value, then your job is to dig in your heels, take everything that you have learned, and use your knowledge to communicate the vision and advise on impactful change. This is a slow and steady immersion in becoming the expert you see yourself as.

Beliefs are no more than thoughts that we have over and over again until they become locked in as truth. While we may be proud to speak of our skills and experience, we may still harbor a deep-rooted set of limiting beliefs that hold us back from our highest potential.

A fear of failure is a common obstacle preventing professionals from growing further in leadership. While they may be excellent at leading their teams to execute projects from start to finish, they don't always feel that their ideas are innovative enough to make a bigger leadership footprint by thinking strategically. Many professionals struggle with a "fraud factor" here, fearing that they could be seen as being in their role for so long that they are unable to redefine themselves and move on. Their work may be proprietary but also have more of a transactional nature to it, that hasn't allowed for much creativity and innovation.

Imagine that you are in a new position that gives you more influence. Where are you now, and where do you see yourself one year from now? What specific experience would you need to gain? Focus only on that experience. Don't get lost in the labels and titles of the ideal leadership opportunity you are looking for. Too many professionals freeze up when they come across a fantastic new opportunity and then fall off their chair after reading the qualifications, especially if the opportunity is in a different industry. They become snowed in by all the buzzwords weaved into the description. Resist the urge to fall into defeat mode. When you sit down and take the time to break down an opportunity, look at those prerequisites for what they mean, underline the industry terms, and unpack the role to understand what it really entails. Instinctually, you should feel whether you have the necessary leadership skills and whether it's an opportunity well within your reach. A strong indicator that you should trust your instincts is if, upon review, you feel that the opportunity would stretch you but not freeze you. If your gut gives you a *yes*, then the opportunity is well worth your further exploration.

When considering a career change with more leadership, don't get snowed in by all the buzzwords in the description of the position. Unpack the role for what it is, and instinctually recognize any fear that builds in you so that you can eliminate it before you react and walk away.

If you're more in the exploratory phase of seeking your next best leadership opportunity, I would coach you to interview for those higher-level positions anyway. Consider it a research and development mission where you can learn what you need to know from the interview, sidebar conversations, and coffee meets to get there in six months to a year. In other words, I'd ask you to work backward. This is a gutsy move because any intuitive hiring manager will see right through the gap in your experience. However, I'd invite you to walk into this discomfort anyway, brush off any embarrassment, and make yourself vulnerable to gain the intelligence you need to understand the gaps so that you can ramp up to filling them. This same approach applies if you took some time off to raise a family and are now reentering the workforce.

Fast-forward six months. You have just stepped into your new role and may not necessarily see yourself as a thought leader; however, this is your lush, freshly cut playing field. At this stage, ask yourself the following questions that will help you develop a mindset to influence change:

"What is our mission, and what vision can I bring to this role?"

"What do I want to have accomplished one year from now? What does success look like?"

"Who will be my best clients and eventual raving fans? Who will most benefit from my work product? To whom should I give my attention?"

"What are their significant pain points that I can alleviate?"

The Midcareer Crisis

Many professionals seeking to move into more leadership halfway through their career recognize in hindsight that their decision to take on more responsibility (e.g., title or compensation) was based on a dangling "carrot" that they believed would ultimately accelerate their career and level of fulfillment. When they seized the opportunity, however, their job satisfaction dropped, and they found themselves asking, "Now what? Did I get what I wanted? If so, then why am I not happy after working myself into the ground to get here?" Often they followed the path laid at their feet. Why would they take any other direction when the natural and assumed next best role was staring them in the face?

Do you know what you want? Ask yourself whether it aligns with what you enjoy and feel enthusiastic about doing. Meet with people who are already in that position so you can be better armed to make a decision that serves you. When you make a career move, how will you know that you have made the right decision?

The answer can be found in a three-step purpose exercise. When you can (1) do what you love doing, (2) use skills that come naturally (i.e., your talents), and (3) accomplish work that feels meaningful to you, that's when you can trust your decision. In other words, your choice is not based on a score to be achieved or a checkbox to be ticked off that you see others doing. It's based on purpose and putting a priority on your level of fulfillment. This is what fuels and furthers your growth and your own desire to inspire and influence others.

This approach requires being willing to act on what is instinctively felt, not seen. There are always alternative paths we can take—a wealth of possibilities circles us all the time. They just aren't always visible, so we don't learn to trust those intuitive hits naturally. Worse, we fear them for the unknown territory and discomfort they embody; yet when we overcome our fear, we somehow always manage and adjust, only to look back and recognize that following our instincts is necessary to our growth.

. You are an expert in your field—keep that present. You do not need to scramble and plan out the next three to five years of your career as a fixed leadership path. It will eventually unfold. Leading from a place where you can see your potential as a leader growing without fixating on what it must look like becomes your point of power.

Here are some titles you can feel free to give yourself as a leader of influence. You're not a technologist, a marketer, a consultant, a business analyst, an educator, an editor, an engineer, an accountant, or a compliance officer. You are a (an):

- Advisor
- Innovator
- Teacher
- Mentor
- Trusted guide
- Expert
- Problem solver
- Results maker
- Specialist
- Solutionist

Which of these titles most resonate with how you see yourself in your field? Even if you have not moved from your current role in several years, self-qualify today as a leading authority there. If you help companies run killer marketing campaigns, then you are a *marketing expert*. If you are great at corporate business development, then your moniker may be *strategic advisor expert*. Become comfortable tagging the word *expert* at the end of your title. Be clear on your guru-ness. It should be noted everywhere, including in your email signature, right next to your contact information.

- Leadership expert for nurse practitioners
- Product development expert for e-commerce solutions
- Instructional design expert for colleges and universities
- Wealth advisor expert for women

At this moment, what's relevant is that you believe you are positioned for growth and can own any one of these monikers. You are no longer valued solely for what you do, even if you have done it brilliantly. Owning your value as a thought leader means that you are recognized for how you think, where you can pull your knowledge and expertise in a given subject area and bundle it into products that you can "sell" to those who need you—your clients. Once you make a mindset shift that embraces this self-assessment, you are free to go on to lead more challenging opportunities, which will position you for more growth, more influence, and more authority.

How will you know when you are ready to step into an opportunity that has the potential for more influence? As humans, we want guarantees.

Deep breathe in.

Exhale.

Intuitively, you will feel it. You will feel ready to grow when you have been on the ground as the quarterback for some time, having enjoyed leading projects and motivating people that now require little effort. With purpose, passion, and a plan, you will know that you are ready to unleash and grow further as a leader. If others seek your advice, guidance, or strategic eye, this speaks to being compensated and recognized as someone who has valuable assets to share and lead with.

There are three roles that leaders have in their career trajectory regardless of the profession or industry in which they work; you can be a basket weaver for a living, and these three roles still apply.

The Three Roles in Your Career Trajectory

Student and Eager Learner

You start out as a *student and eager learner,* where you learn the ropes and all the benefits of your work practice from being on the ground in execution mode. With sleeves rolled up, you are hands-on, doing a thorough amount of research, studying, training, and possibly being mentored along the way. You become brilliant at understanding the ins and outs of your role and have both feet planted firmly on the ground. This stage of your career is when you were essentially a human sponge.

Teacher and Results Maker

In one year, you have perfected that first role. You have become so good at it that you are the quarterback who supports others in accomplishing their projects. You become the person who knows how to motivate and get the job done. By hook or by crook, you can deliver on results. Should you ever become stuck, you instinctively know how you and/or your team can figure it out or will find a resource that does. Should someone ever hit a wall and require your graceful intervention, there, too, you will make the much-needed phone call to push things along. You continue to move your feet and be of service. You learn to shimmy your way through any complex problem and aren't averse to getting your hands dirty at times to support the greater whole. You are accustomed to rolling up your sleeves solo or with your team and tackling the unknown to deliver on your commitments.

You are a *teacher and results maker* at this stage. If you are called on to train or advise someone, you share all the little nuances you've learned to help that person work smarter and make his or her job easier. You can quickly point your learners to the red flags, what to watch out for and how to develop more elegant solutions. You also freely show them your little-known backdoor strategies to get around problems as the results maker and go-giver you are.

Advisor and Role Model

You have become so good at what you do that you are considered a trusted *advisor and role model.* You enjoy connecting the dots for others and no longer speak solely to improvements in a specific business area. Instead, you enjoy talking to the rationale behind why things are done the way they are and how best practices and standards can be applied across other arms of the business. Your focus is on the future vision with a close eye on positive, impactful change for those best clients and raving fans you've corralled along the way.

Given all your experience, problems don't surface; there is only creative thinking to come up with innovative solutions. This mantra you pass on when mentoring others as well. You look to hire those who think creatively and learn your role better than you, fondly recalling being in their same shoes all those years ago. You understand that the best leaders are those who can lead and also be led.

Can you see why thought leadership is a natural milestone on your career path? Why else have you worked so hard to get where you are today, if not to package up all your expert wisdom to serve in a bigger way? This applies if you're transitioning to a new industry, market, or business area. Wherever you go, leverage all your business experience, because it adds up to the value inside your career leadership portfolio. You have built a reputation as an expert who doesn't just participate in the conversation, sharing good advice, but who also now *drives* it.

Four Stages of Growth

There is a well-accepted learning theory that is whispered in the learning model of psychology. All humans have a star they're shooting for, a personal success mission, if you will—whatever they have defined that as. Psychologists indicate that no matter what you set out to learn or be as either a child or an adult, there are four core learning stages you must pass through if you're resilient enough. Turning these stages into calls to action is easier said than done but well worth it if you are ready to learn the skills to get you where you want to be (most people give up somewhere around stage 2½).

Stage 1: Unconscious Incompetence

This is the stage where you have no insight on how to do something, and here's the rub: you are not even aware that you are incapable. You rebuff any value in learning a new skill to achieve success and lean on the skills that you do have. This may be deemed a *stagnation stage* because you are knee-deep in denial. Until you accept its relevance, you will be unable to move on to stage 2.

Stage 2: Conscious Incompetence

Here your eyes are wide open. You recognize that you don't know how to do something but that it is relevant to what you are trying to achieve. You have unquestionably turned over a new leaf and are eager to keep failing until you learn the new skills well.

Stage 3: Conscious Competence

You are now swimming in the deep end of the pool. Not only have you learned how to perform the skills you need, but you are working on perfecting them. You are in deep concentration but still taking baby steps to get there. Ever the eternal and eager learner, you continue on, taking a slow and steady approach.

Stage 4: Unconscious Competence

You have had so much hands-on practice that these skills are now second nature. You are ready to pay it forward, teaching others your wisdom and essential lessons learned. You have accepted your failures and continue to look for new ways to improve, which includes investing in others because you have further developed your expertise from investing in yourself.

Which stage are you at in your career? If it's anything less than stage 4, what would have to happen for you to get there? Instinctively, what would you need right now to grow further?

The Go-to Catch-22

It can be somewhat of a burden for you to be the designated resource from whom others are always seeking answers and yet for you to still continue to learn and grow in your own career. On the one hand, you may feel appreciated as the go-to resource, with raised confidence to have established a name and reputation for yourself. On the other hand, as a leader destined for more opportunity, you can also pigeon-hole yourself if you remain where you are for too long or, worse, become so comfortable that you never want to leave, losing those raving fans to go somewhere else. Either way, it's not sustainable. It's likely time to cultivate a team of go-to gurus.

Let's unpack being that go-to leader some more. The very reason people gravitate to you is that you go above and beyond to benefit the whole—the team, the project, the department, and ultimately the organization. You operate from a place of service, and now you want to move on and take on more challenging responsibilities that offer more exposure or maybe pivot in a different direction and embrace new endeavors. Please take a moment to celebrate yourself. It's a gutsy move to own your self-worth. Stay the course with focus; your instincts will fully support you on this path.

Let's revisit your personal brand and value proposition, because it's time for you to bundle all your expertise as a product. This is where you leverage to reach a new level of influence. You have already built a reputation for yourself as a one-stop solution for others who seek your expertise. Looking at your life holistically, you may even find patterns on a personal level where you volunteer to be the default driver at home as well, often relied on to get the job done rather than encouraging others to come up with their own solutions.

Not surprisingly, most professionals who land leadership positions have built a reputation for being the quarterback because they have been so versatile that they take on any new projects thrown their way. Inevitably this too comes with a heavy burden—all roads now lead to you.

GROWING PAINS ARE THE WAKE-UP CALL

It's a natural rite of passage: Why wouldn't you want to go from being the subject matter expert to leading a bigger team or new business practice, division, or department? In contrast, it can be painful to make a move. Rationally, you may understand that you need to be consistently uncomfortable to grow, but let's not forget that as humans, we are also creatures of comfort. You may resist making the mental shift involved in going from thinking that enhances execution of deliverables to planning bigger based on a broader vision.

Thoughts of not being strategic, articulate, or confident enough at times can crop up. These are limiting beliefs that will bubble up at every turn. This is your ego doing its job to protect you from playing too big and part of human growth. Fear can't be eliminated; our primal ancestors needed fear to survive, and that's why we have evolved to where we are today. You can, however, use the necessary tools to address fear as if it's sitting in the room right next to you as a third party and act anyway *despite* the fear. Whenever you feel that impulse to act, that's something you can trust and is worth following through on. This is why intuition is the greatest decision-making tool we have been afforded as human beings. Intuition can be particularly powerful when you are facing unforeseen circumstances that offer little in the way of facts or basic data on which you can rely. During times like these, when you're under pressure to perform, your decisions cannot be pulled directly from reason or based on any real evidence to substantiate your choices. Success, however, leaves a footprint. Intuition can be based on certain decisions and how they compare with past successful outcomes that share similar patterns. These patterns can bolster a sense of familiarity that evokes a trust in following your instincts.

Here are some facts you can trust. There are years of satisfaction and pride behind your excellent command of operations, either from supporting an organization or in front-facing roles such as navigating sales teams. It also takes an enormous amount of mental energy to get unstuck when you are trapped in the predictability of new projects and have outgrown where you are. Intellectually, you need to be challenged, or you will not thrive. Your predictable routine now makes mornings monotonous, draining your energy and mental strength as you walk into work each day. You can become glued to and complacent with what you know despite your instinct to move on. It is precisely when you reach this flatlined stage in your career that your instinct begs you to move on.

If you were to look back at any difficult situation in your life, you might see that there were always one or two blinking warning signs flagging you to slow down. Choosing to ignore these yellow alerts can turn into years of unhappiness; yet why do we still move ahead?

Usually, you'll find that there is always a payoff. You may be clear on the cost, but what did you gain? Choosing to remain where you are is comfortable. You may have done well in your career, worked hard, had a steady income, had ample flexibility to raise a family, and justified your value as a relied-on leader for years. Why mess with a good thing, right? Not so. If you're not waking up daily willing to be uncomfortable, how can you experience a desired change?

Imagine, instead, that you are already in your desired new role. Take a mental picture of transitioning to more leadership using all five senses. What does it look like? How does it feel? The more you lock in those desired images in your mind, the more opportunities will meet you at the door. Keep refining your vision, responding to questions to give you clarity such as the following:

- How many people are on your team?
- Do you regularly sit in a boardroom?
- What are your peers like?
- Do you lead companywide talks and presentations?
- What kind of work are you doing that feels meaningful? How do you feel leading your one-on-ones? What concerns do you listen for?
- What kind of relationships do you consistently build? Are they more internal or external to your organization?

Journal your responses as you lean in further to these kinds of prompts; your responses are what you desire and help shape the images that you want to experience in your next opportunity. More importantly, these are your intentions that will help you focus through your mind's eye, strengthening your instincts. When preparing for a career transition, it's a nonnegotiable to put those intentions out there. If you don't feel like you belong where you are any longer, visualize working somewhere else—a place that is a perfect fit—leading with your expertise and your ability to deliver value. Your only job at this stage is to let go and truly feel that new experience.

> When there is no oil left in your lamp, you have no light left. With ample space and time to focus, that's when you achieve clarity on what's meaningful and instinctually what that next best step is that you should take.

Something transformational happens when you speak of the things that you want out loud. It creates energy that others will feel based on your belief in yourself, and this picks up momentum quickly. You have the power to unlock your highest potential when you tap into that higher vision you've designed for yourself. It activates the power of focus and is why writing your goals down has an extraordinary ability to attract the right people, opportunities, and resources to support you. You have locked into your mind what it is you truly want and are able to feel what the new state is like. It's the feeling that matters. Writing morning pages is a powerful mental practice that can help you to accomplish this vision. First introduced in *The Artist's Way*, by Julia Cameron, the idea is that by writing three pages a day as a stream of consciousness, you can unblock your creativity and expand thinking. She refers to these pages as a tool that helps you "get to the other side" between the logic brain and the artist brain. "Logic brain is our brain of choice in the western hemisphere. . . . Anything unknown is perceived as wrong and possibly dangerous. Artist brain is our inventor and inner child." This process can be compared with picking up the phone and calling yourself each morning. Over time, the pages you write lead to a deepening sense of inner wisdom and courage to describe a vision you have chosen for yourself by sharing it with others. This not only increases the likelihood that you will achieve your vision but also ensures that you hold yourself committed and accountable at the same time.

When we are sedentary for too long, sitting on our hands waiting, we feel stuck and stagnant, which is not a natural human state. In this state, growth stops. It's why, at times, you may feel as though you can no longer breathe. Being in motion and acting on instinctual thoughts give you momentum, where you find yourself feeling enthusiastic, making progress toward the things you want and believe are possible. Once you step into this higher awareness of possibility, you can't turn back. If you tried, you would feel as though you had taken two steps back, and you would suddenly find inner resistance because you have already expanded your vision.

We always know when we are ready for more leadership; yet for some reason, we don't always give ourselves permission to really know. We become weighed down by limiting beliefs and a glass-half-empty perspective, having no trouble pointing out the imperceptible flaws and nicks that substantiate why something may not be possible for us.

What you instinctively feel is what drives that bigger vision you've created for yourself—your highest potential. When you look back at the moments that held the most joy in your life, these were the times when your energy was light and playful. In these experiences, you were aligned with who you are. Instinct is often referred to as an entity inside your body; yet it's the other way around. You are energy that happens to have a physical form—your physical body.

Cherished memories reflect moments when you felt free from any constraints. When you are in a free-flowing state, that's when you are in a high-energy field and can always trust your instincts when making critical decisions. Those thoughts are guiding you in the direction where you are meant to go.

LEADERSHIP, NOT MANAGEMENT

Many professionals indicate that while they want more influence and recognition, they want to steer clear of a role that beckons a management path. Higher-level leadership roles are perceived to come with a price—more stress, more pressure to perform, more responsibility and hence room for failure, and more face time in exchange for more compensation and a weighty title. The same mindset can show up for small-business owners when reflecting on having a flourishing company. They are concerned about losing quality time with family and the things they enjoy in exchange for more income and success. An attractive proposition, however, may not be entirely worth the price they want to pay.

Not everyone is destined for management, and there are plenty of professionals who are perfectly happy to remain leading inside their expert domain. There's no shame or blame in this. If, however, you have reached a point where performing your role is draining your best energy and mental strength and you feel that itch to move on, don't sell yourself short: management is only one path you can take.

Managing is not in itself traditional leadership. It is not vision, inspiring others, gaining buy-in, encouraging creativity, or instilling change. Managerial leadership, however, is a combination of having the skills of a manager and the qualities of a leader. Being an effective manager requires leadership that focuses your energies on goals that solve problems and on how people and processes can "play" and operate together to achieve specific results for the organization.

Professionals without any direct reports sometimes can demonstrate leadership skills that are even better than those of professionals with a formal management title next to their names. Leadership requires influence—being able to influence thoughts and actions in people. You can, for example, lead a team collaborating in a flat-level organization that is peer to peer. For many people, this can feel like an excellent and safer leap into leadership versus that compulsory next level up, which feels more like a cliffside jump.

Practicing your ability to bring people together will always be a priority and critical metric, irrespective of whether you have direct reports. How included do you make people feel? Inclusion must be felt everywhere, and it's how good leaders increase their influence—by establishing trust.

Training others and being in an advisory role are other opportunities where you can package and disseminate your expert knowledge to grow in leadership. Creating a curriculum, building a model, and providing a best practices guide that's proved to work are all avenues to remain in service using your expertise as a proven advisor. If you have domain leadership, you are a specialist who can serve stakeholders and constituents without managing anyone directly while still enjoying your best work and doing what you love.

Many executives turned managing directors share that they have felt some pressure taking that next expected position on their career path. This same mindset and unspoken expectation particularly applies to the law profession: "Either I make partner soon, or I become a liability and my career flatlines forever."

It's a natural response to choose the fixed path defined by your industry, but what if you could design a position that works for you and your family? Don't put pressure on yourself if, given your age or years of experience, you must make a move by industry standards. Speak regularly with people in management at company functions and external resources in your industry to pick their brains so that you have a clear picture of what the prospect of transitioning to something new would look like. Leading with influence can mean moving laterally to new functional areas or staying put and taking on more responsibilities with a new set of clients from another business area, designing a role that challenges you and you enjoy *on your own terms*. This also bridges the gap where you can learn and absorb the business methods of leaders in other units, and they, in turn, can learn from you by being present to your expert business domain. This is a win-win all around, bringing different mindsets together to round out your knowledge while supporting you and allowing you to grow in your organization.

Knowing how to get things done is important, but sharing that knowledge is what is most impactful and is how you widen your playing field. What you deliver does not have to be perfect (it rarely is). Any speaker who makes a lucrative income inspiring people will say that each time he or she shows up on stage (or teaches or consults), the content is never perfect. These speakers consistently grow by connecting with their audiences, learning from the question-and-answer slots, and then correcting course, refining, tweaking, and producing their next best talk based on the feedback. As an intrapreneur inside an organization, you are always learning, and I'd venture to say that as a lifelong learner, you are wired with a desire to teach others as well, helping them grow.

For some reason, however, as we advance in our careers, we tend to want to be the human sponge that absorbs all the knowledge we need overnight so that we can answer any question thrown our way. This is unrealistic misplaced energy that will not serve you. It also sends a clear message that there is no wiggle room for you to make mistakes. This self-inflicted pressure will trickle down to everyone and is how negative cultures develop. As a leader, how will you nurture a culture and a team that will grow? What do you want your leadership legacy to be?

No man will make a great leader who wants
to do it all themself or gets all the credit for doing it.
ANDREW CARNEGIE

When you think about your people, the team you want to work with, what message do you want to convey? Will they be allowed to make mistakes if you have raised the perfection paralysis bar so high for yourself? When you consider the kind of support structure you want in place, including the people you lead, do you create a safe and trusted space? Taken too far, aiming for pristine results tends to slow people and processes down, which inevitably has an impact on the entire team.

Those who work with you will only grow as far as you've allowed yourself to grow. This is why it's so essential for us as leaders, parents, peers, and partners to allow ourselves to make mistakes, so that we can keep growing in our relationships. Others may not always agree with your ideas, but they will always respect you because they recognize themselves in you when you take the time to ramp up and learn what you need to grow.

As a leader, you are continually learning, teaching, and growing—guided instinctively by your vision. You will find that there are several doorways to opportunities when you are the results maker. If your clients love your energy, humor, wittiness, even temper, and patience, then keep the good going. Your work and how you deliver it will find a home and speak for itself.

> *I don't necessarily have to like my players,*
> *but as their leader, I must love them.*
> *Love is loyalty, love is teamwork,*
> *love respects the dignity of the individual.*
> *This is the strength of any organization.*
> VINCE LOMBARDI

FIND A VOID AND FILL IT

> *A pessimist sees the difficulty in every opportunity;*
> *an optimist sees the opportunity in every difficulty.*
> WINSTON S. CHURCHILL

There is an unspoken vault of overlooked opportunities in every organization. They are always voids that require a rescue or rebuild mission. You know only too well where these voids are because they eventually find solution-driven experts like you to pick up their cause. They are the communication gaps growing wider because of departmental silos. They are process flow inefficiencies. They are superiors who lack planning ability and leadership. They are misplaced management priorities compared with the practical realities that teams are facing. They are a leader's failure to listen to his or her team. They are employees who lack training. And the list goes on and on.

These muddy waters will keep a business unit and team from being successful. You, however, as the subject matter expert, have an up-front picture of what those voids are, and by flagging them down, you now have a ripe opportunity to influence and institute change.

> Have you heard of challenges faced by others and discovered ways you
> can solve their problems? Have you seen how a change in one department
> or function can impact and improve another? Could you throw together
> an impromptu meeting to address these problems? Leaders of influence
> become brilliant at finding voids to fill.

Having a pulse on any one of these problems is what triggers conversations where you can home in on and highlight changes that are desperately needed while at the same time leveraging your expertise. You drive decisions when you speak up and make recommendations on new resources, stopgaps, prospective clients, suppliers, or technologies. When someone like you understands the challenges and can speak to how to address them, you are leading with influence. Keep in mind that you are suggesting the support and expertise needed to get the job done; you and your team are not the designated fixer-uppers. When people come to you for answers or how-to advice, you are not their problem solver. You are a decision maker. You have a keen ear for listening to recurring patterns and communication breakdowns. You help people think through what needs to happen without implying that your business corner can fix what needs to happen. This is an important distinction to make when offering guidance to others.

Success is where preparation and opportunity meet.
BOBBY UNSER

Sometimes, those in positions of authority encourage building barriers, protecting their turf from other departments, often embodying an us-versus-them approach. This can become a challenge if you want to be an effective leader and establish trust with your constituents. Somewhere down the line, you must have demonstrated leadership because you were placed in your current role. You were not hired to be the designated *yes* person but someone who is in a position to lead, think independently, and make decisions. Creating engagement and collaboration with your clients and business partners will support your success in that role versus a command-and-control leadership style.

The command-and-control leadership mindset is an old-school top-down leadership approach that prefers tight control over people. Usually, such an approach to leadership results in an inability to complete projects because there simply aren't enough resources or a big enough budget to go around, and all this is always rooted in fear. Short-term wins may be achieved but at the expense of more impactful initiatives that you could otherwise lead on your watch. Building walls and creating interdepartmental silos do not set either you or your team up for success in the long run because you will never be empowered to be effective at leading anyone. While you might please your direct managers by following their approach, should you take a territorial stance, as a product of that organization, you can negatively impact your business relationships. You also won't sell yourself as well as you could have if you had remained true to your principles while owning your personal authority and reputation.

These are the times when you want to listen to your instincts—not when everything is running smoothly, but when you are called to make the tough decisions that lean in a gray area. What does your gut say? Your choice will be based on your belief that despite management feedback encouraging you to adopt the command style, you can still achieve results that are authentically aligned with your core values.

If you have many years of experience that you can leverage to advance your leadership, where should you start? Keep it simple.

Start with your low-hanging fruit—the clients in other business areas on whom your team ideally could make the most impact, delivering meaningful results. Begin with proven results that have worked in the past, and package them as your next opportunity. This is your hook, even if you have mentally checked out of the very role that positioned you to gain the experience you need in this situation in the first place. Consider it your company's return on its investment in you. Be aware of where the traps are. Speak to what worked in the past and what now needs to change. Speak to the pitfalls that became apparent and the rescue missions that saved a project or program. Speak to the clients who will benefit the most from your work product and who have the potential to become your raving fans. They are the people who are listening to you because they know that they can benefit from the results you promise. The only prerequisites for this approach to work are that you must know your clients and feel passionate about instituting change. Inspiring energy will mobilize others into action every time. Don't be surprised on this growth journey that you discover that you have a strong desire to empower others, where, instinctively, you feel called to help others succeed, clearing any roadblocks from their path.

Know Thy Customer

Whenever someone shares with me his or her good news about a recent career move, my first question after the celebration winds down is always the same: "What's next? Fast-forward one year from now. Where do you want to be?"

Now the person may respond, "Hold on, Marisa. I've just started in this new leadership role. I need time to figure that out."

You are always looking for your next opportunity. If you're not strategic about where you are headed, how will you know how to get there? How will you know what you should focus on to be successful, including which clients you should give the most attention to—your low-hanging fruit? Low-hanging fruit also includes those outside of your organization who may have expressed genuine interest in you and in learning more about what you do. People who you meet at networking or industry events may very well have the potential to be *future* clients.

If you know who your key clients are and what they need, including your own management, then you are their number one service provider. You can then become clear about why you and your team are the best consultants to address their problems. When it comes to your boss, this is "managing up" by anticipating what priorities your boss has, and what his or her triggers are that should be avoided. Put yourself in other people's shoes; see what they see. Give them your undivided attention. This not only engages them but also builds a lifetime of trust. It's a love story like no other when you can meet them where they are with a return on results.

What would your constituents want from you that would be of value to them? Why should they give you their time? How will your proposals make a difference? How will you measure their success? What plan B will you reassure them with and put in place if all else fails?

Find a void and fill it. What results do you promise? Keep in mind that you couldn't commit to making any promises had you not taken the time to understand your clients' challenges. Instinctively, this is why you know that you are qualified to lead and influence them. Subconsciously, everyone wants to be led. Your managers want you to lead them. They want to sleep well at night knowing that you have their backs.

At any stage when you are seeking to grow in leadership and have more influence, question why things are run the way they are and show how you can contribute to positive change. If you visit any business site online, you can immediately see what products are being pushed and promoted; the same exposure applies to your career. If you choose to remain in your organization, how can you get more exposure to what's going on in the front-facing side of the business? Who is a strong contact who can connect you?

Impact and Improve Mindset

Assume that you have just been asked to wing a presentation that needs buy-in from your stakeholders. You have five minutes to prepare. This call to action should require no rehearsal because you will always find the right words when you're leading from instinct. Is this a guarantee that you can make this contribution in such a short amount of time? Here's a systematic approach that will support you in delivering that proposal in no time, securing buy-in every time:

1. Put yourself in your clients' shoes. Rather than talk about what you do, approach this opportunity by talking about the results you and/or your team can deliver first. Talk about your clients' benefits. Walk them through the transformation. Although your clients may deeply respect you and your work, they don't want to hear about you or what processes you have put in place. They want to understand why your proposal matters to them in their work lives. In other words, pretend that the only question taped to their foreheads is, "So what?"
2. Present three topics that you wish to highlight and discuss.
3. For each topic, consider three reasons why what you are presenting matters—that is, the *why*. Why does your proposal matter? Educate your clients on the three biggest mistakes they should avoid. Show them the three biggest obstacles that they are not aware of and that are standing in their way. How would your recommendations institute change?
4. Harness this thought stream by capturing the results you guarantee if your clients follow your lead: Result 1, Result 2, Result 3, and so on. These are the promises that you are making.
5. Fluff it up with a personal story at the beginning and end of your presentation, and close with any questions.

Five minutes of pure instinctual action and you are done. You influence change when you can succinctly walk others through your ideas, keeping their needs and results in mind with full transparency and commitment.

If you follow this approach to securing buy-in, you can later flesh it out in a subsequent five-slide deck. Why would your customers care? What's in it for them? Work backward with the results and return on investment and rest assured that your presentation will flow. This approach naturally prepares you for any pushback questions that could blindside you. Preparation meets opportunity when you keep your eye on the results, speaking your constituents' language and understanding their challenges.

Your know-how will speak for itself when you instinctively focus on your clients' needs, pain points, and struggles. You gain buy-in and make an even stronger case when you seed your ideas with those of your team, allow them to improve your approach, and then step back, remain flexible, and trust when others disagree. Let your wing men and women punch holes in your presentation so that you can refine and perfect it further before socializing your strategy to your base of raving fans.

A good rule of thumb: if you can't explain your proposal, project, or program simply and concisely enough for a newcomer or freshman to understand, then your message needs to be reworked. This is how digestible and clear anything that you are speaking on or presenting should be. When communicating your vision, first get it out of your head and on paper so that it makes sense to you. Speak it out loud to see if you're presenting something that's 30,000 feet above ground level or you have landed the plane for your listeners and have covered their needs.

Many leaders overlook answering the "So what?" question. They don't take the time to help their clients understand why their ideas and recommendations are relevant. They assume that explaining *what* they are proposing and *how* they will approach it is the best way to influence. However, this is actually a missed opportunity because it may only be self-evident to them and not to their clients, who might miss the point entirely without being given an explanation or roadmap as to why it matters and will ultimately impact *them*.

How Do You Build Trust?

Communicating the *why* is where successful leaders break ground and establish trust with their clients and teams. If you listen closely to any strong salesperson, you will find that he or she consistently talks about the transformation, not the process. Strong salespeople focus on the results that their products guarantee. They treat sales as service. They talk about the before and after states from hiring or buying from them. They speak with confident clarity so that their customers have no doubt about how their product or service will change their lives. When you focus on how you want people to feel in your relationships, you effectively drive your mutual results, forming trusted partnerships. Your clients want to feel that you have their backs. They also want to know that you understand their pain points and can speak their language. You establish trust by speaking as if you are in their shoes and understand them. You can finish their sentences for them and bring their purpose straight home when you speak on their behalf, socializing their mission. In some cases, you may have actually been in their shoes, substantiating further why you are qualified to speak from a place of authority.

WII FM Radio

WII FM stands for "What's in it for me?" and this is the one radio station that everyone is always dialed into, including you in this moment. When you lead anyone on any subject matter, it's natural to think, "I want to walk away with this, or I need them to sign off on that." Do you hear how it's all about *you* in there?

You can't be aware of others' challenges and be in those conversations, listening to their pain points and ultimately coming from a place of service, unless you raise your hand and ask questions about their corner of the world. This involves having a solid appreciation of where others are and how you can help even if you play a small role in their bigger picture. It might even mean referring them to someone else if you're not the best resource and being fully transparent about that standing in integrity. This outreach is also how you are able to figure people out in an altruistic way, allowing them to relax because they feel that you understand them.

In order to gather the intelligence you need and ultimately bring value to your role, you must bring a curious mind to the conversation. However, leaders sometimes beat themselves up if they don't have the magic bullet that answers every question, but this is not what matters most to people. When people feel appreciated, they allow themselves to be led. When you open up a conversation that makes your clients feel safe trusting that you have considered what it's like to be in their shoes, they can relax and begin to explore new avenues of growth with you.

What are your clients' hot buttons? What are their daily struggles? What keeps them up at night? Your goal is to have them breathing easy. Tuning to WII FM radio is a constant assessment of being in other people's shoes, not just your own, and discovering how you can support them first. It's listening to the story behind the story when someone speaks. It's listening to what's not being said, as much as what is.

Successful leaders not only activate keen listening skills in this way but also empower others to feel included and have their voices heard in the room. You can mold to different personalities who stand apart from your own style. You can comfortably partner with someone who tends to be high strung as much as someone who is more reserved and tends to hold back before instilling trust in someone.

Owning your authority involves initiating conversations by hearing what the needs are and how you can help while remaining intentional to why you are there—the very motivation for why you do what you do. This kind of self-awareness is how you drive transformation and, under your leadership, motivate others (including your team) to do the same.

How included you make people in the room feel drives how successful you are. People may not always remember your face or where they met you, but they will never forget how they felt around you and what their first instincts were about you.

You were born with a desire for love and acceptance—these are two of our most fundamental needs. This is also why being of service to others and acting on purpose fulfill those desires. There's no secret sauce on how to lead with influence. It's a two-part formula that consists of one part giving and one part receiving.

How do you give with an open spirit? Be curious with your clients. Ask what they need. In any conversation, meeting, or phone call, make a mindset shift about why you are there. When you speak up by asking questions, you see the world through another's lens before aiming for any quick wins that would solely benefit you. When you are comfortable putting yourself inside that kind of conversation, you are being present and will experience a dynamic shift in your relationship, opening yourself up to new opportunities and levels of influence.

The Multiplier Effect

Great leaders want others to take their ideas and feel inspired to "plus" them—create improvements on top of their best practices. As someone who educates and provides value, you'll often find that others on your team will want to run with ideas when they are clearly communicated. Here you are empowering them to own their authority and make them even better.

When you create a space for others to "plus" your work, you become, in effect, a *multiplier*. Multipliers share new concepts that others can run with to improve and perfect, unlike leaders considered diminishers, who sweep their teams' ideas to the side. Good leaders position themselves as multipliers by including others in the conversation and allowing them to multiply their results and scale.

The strategy of leading as a multiplier is rooted in "mastermind groups," first introduced by Napoleon Hill in his book *Think and Grow Rich*.[1] Hill describes a group of two or more people in which each participant shares a like-minded thought that he or she wouldn't typically have developed on his or her own if not for the group dynamic. He goes on to share that American steel tycoon Andrew Carnegie "attributed his entire fortune on the power he accumulated through this 'Master Mind.' Mr. Carnegie's Master Mind group consisted of a staff of approximately fifty men, with whom he surrounded himself, for the definite purpose of manufacturing and marketing steel."

Today, masterminds are meant to present, discuss, collaborate, and gain feedback where everyone at the table is asked to commit verbally to something by the meeting's end. You, too, can bring that creative energy to a room by encouraging a "meeting of the minds" that expands on ideas and the trust others have in following your lead.

MASTER SMART AND SIMPLE

If you have always thrived on absorbing and analyzing information, are highly organized, and can easily form patterns around how different functions operate, keep the good going because these skills pay off in your career. If you are someone who can master tasks easily "in your sleep" and embody critical-thinking skills, you will appreciate that thought leadership is a continuation of that process. When you develop any step-by-step approach or best practice that has positively impacted or improved an area of business, once again, this is your trigger to package and institutionalize it. This is your opportunity to bundle your product and bring it to light using straightforward, no-frills language that people can easily digest and retain.

Leading with influence is consistently disseminating your best practices to create and market your results in the form of self-promotion (as discussed in Chapter 1). Marketing your message in this way also avoids the potential of sharing too much information, which inevitably can have those seeking your inputs flounder from *analysis paralysis*. Successful leaders will bundle their expert method by filtering out the noise and disseminating the right information to the right people at the right time and then will let go, allowing others on their teams to run with it and enhance it even further.

> You cultivate your personal brand by building credibility as an expert who no longer participates in the conversation but now drives it, allowing others to shine and perfect it further.

Let's examine the areas where you have observed the work of others and have developed your own solutions and methods that helped them to work smarter. You demonstrate your value by taking those solutions and speaking to them in any setting—formal meetings or casual chitchat. The soft skill of advising with simplified solutions drives candid conversations and offers full transparency on how things can be done better.

Intuitive Business Documents

Providing information that is relevant—and timely—to people throughout an organization is a leadership asset that develops the cornerstone for building your center of excellence (COE), further increasing your impact. Such information typically takes the form of business documents on which your clients rely, ranging from compliance red flags to organizational governance. The information also can consist of clearly outlined systemized routines that have been put in place or business requirements that have been sequenced together in an enterprise-wide plan. Your team can use this information to transform chaos to calm by instituting best practices that others can build on. Other business groups will be grateful if you can simplify the places where they should focus their efforts; they can save hours of time simply by following practical guides that run like a well-oiled machine. You'll find that sharing any information that provides a clear path using metrics is an asset that the right business partners will appreciate and eagerly digest.

These intuitive business documents can span across siloed business units and product lines and in some way educate and support others. Under your leadership, your team can churn out white papers, elegant process flows and integrations, product definitions, client needs analyses, dictionaries, and even visual representations that focus on a value-added story involving any corner of the business.

You may become so proficient as a leading expert that it's easy to forget what it took to get there. Mindset shift: not everyone knows what you know. Some people may just be coming in as a new member of a team or from another area of the business. So when you see the question marks coming in, you instinctively know that it's time to provide a new leadership asset that supports others in performing their jobs well.

Writing these offerings may not always be desirable because of the time investment they require. Yet they are the communication vehicles that allow you to share critical information in an insightful simple way, ultimately educating your audience. Keep in mind that it's not enough to simply develop and circulate digestible artifacts for others to understand. Owning your authority is taking responsibility for sharing your knowledge and best practices—and here, too, marketing your value.

EDUCATION, NOT EGO

If you fish for others, you only feed them for a day.
If you teach them how to fish, you feed them for a lifetime.
LAO TZU

If you consider yourself a credible expert who can cut through the noise for others and deliver something well worth focusing on, saving them time or effort, then, here again, consider yourself to be a thought leader in your industry. Unfortunately, there may be times when you hold yourself back from speaking about your proven systems and true concerns that address the elephant in the room. This is not because you're unsure of whether you're good enough, despite your ego attempting to keep you feeling small. It's that sometimes you may worry about whether you will not be perceived confidently and appear not to know what you're talking about. This is because you may not have every answer or, worse, you may wing it to a potential place of embarrassment. Your inner crow will try to take you down at every turn. Rest assured, the ego is toying with you, doing its job to protect you, which, as a side effect, will pull you down with limiting beliefs.

Authentic leaders are wired to share what they know, whether with a recommendation or a best practice. Therefore, instinctually, fall back to an unemotional, matter-of-fact approach that clearly says, "Here's what I know. Here's what I don't know. Here's what I know that works."

Does it matter that what you are sharing is laid out in the finest minute detail? Do you need to run every proposal by everyone for watertight validation before you're allowed to bring it to a wider audience? A resounding *no*.

What you know is based on experience as well as instinct. You can make a split-second decision based on a go-for-broke approach, where there are few options, time is running out, and the unpopular plan B must kick in. Although including your team and seeking input from peers are important, you don't require them before making a final decision. While feedback is essential for effective leadership, not all feedback is a *fait accompli*. This is freedom like no other when you consider how you own your authority.

There's no rhyme or reason to trust your gut other than being self-aware of your emotions. Do you feel nervous or any fear? Hold the line if those two emotions are dominant. You don't want to make a decision from that place. If, in contrast, you feel the excitement and nervousness of a positive expected outcome, go for it. You're not interpreting a crystal ball; you're using your internal guidance based on a combination of emotion and logic, which will help you to make the best decision you can at the time, and with the information you have synthesized.

Lead your clients with what you know has worked, avoiding what you have personally found will not work—based on your expert opinion and instinct. Trusted advisors lead with high intention and low attachment—they purposefully share their expertise and then let go, confident in their recommendations and proposals because they stand behind them. They believe in them. Whether your ideas are accepted is irrelevant; don't get caught up on the receiving end. What matters is that you say what you believe at the time based on the facts, feedback, data, and any number of other factors presented to you. Beliefs are thoughts that you have over and over again until they become locked in your mind as truth. Strong beliefs instill confidence, which creates energy that people feel and want for themselves. Confidence develops resilience and makes us feel alive—and the world needs more leaders who are *alive.*

You can't be everything for everyone. Your ego wants you to be liked at all times. Your ego wants to be placed on a pedestal, glowing with the satisfaction of facing any size audience with pride. However, as a leader, your goal is not to please people. It's to be respected and have your ideas valued. Otherwise, everyone would fall into a one-size-fits-all leadership style that, in the end, suits no one. Your proven systems create your leadership footprint. The more people you teach to clone and multiply your work, the larger is the impact you have—that's how you lead with influence and own your authority.

Draw Out the Bigger Vision

Many of the best ideas fail when business leaders propose only a short-term life span for a program, say six to nine months, which may be the current focus. While your clients may appreciate you framing up what's happening now, what they need from you, even more so, is to lay out a multiyear roadmap: "When are we doing what? What is the bigger vision, and what is the long-term impact that will benefit us and the organization as a whole?"

You don't need to be working on a cure for cancer to validate your vision. Anything you pitch will stick and be well received as long as its motivation is to serve your clients and keep their best interests in mind. Trust your instincts; the direction you outline should be solid and good enough even if you leave the organization in one year and will not see the project through to completion. Owning your authority, you are hitting areas of consideration needed in the long run: "How much time will it take? How much will it cost? What are the dependencies to plan for?"

Suppose that you are a health coach working with someone who wants to lose 50 pounds in nine months. As the nutrition expert you are, you can get your client to that goal, but what's next after those nine months are through? What if your client now needs someone to keep him or her accountable to an exercise regimen, say one hundred sit-ups three times a week?

There's always going to be a "What's next?" question in the back of your clients' minds. As a business leader, the answer lies in you painting that future vision and mapping out how your plan can help your clients get there. Sharing a program's themes can also function as a roadmap depicting an exact timeline of *what's* happening *when.*

Let's go back to you, the hypothetical health coach. What if you give your client a timeline to follow in his or her cooking and nutrition habits in the first six months and then transition to a fitness regimen in the next half of the year. This could later turn into a time and stress management program. New products, more value. See how it works?

Mindset shift—you're not a one-hit wonder. You are a long-term investment whose return on results is not based solely on what you deliver today but on what you promise for tomorrow—that long-term vision. Lead your managers, peers, prospects, and business partners by walking them through the entire path they should take, from day one through to the long term.

Once you present a long-term plan that showcases the themes and benefits, your team can always circle back and fill in the details of the framework it needs to get into motion. Establish priorities as you move along with your team, and reuse that blueprint later in your next role.

First, you speak strategy; then, you whittle down to the details. You don't have to reinvent systems that already exist. There will always be new initiatives, and certainly, not everything will be "lift and shift." However, using this approach makes it easier to take well-thought-out actions and address contingencies to help you leverage one program to another. Influencing change gets so much easier over time when you consistently leverage your best work.

What's Your Plan B?

In a world of uncertainty, with every strategy you pitch, don't lose sight of the fallback plan. Discussion of potential failure doesn't come up naturally in meetings; yet the threat of any risk inevitably will lead to exposure. Good business leaders consider the what-ifs before pulling the trigger.

This mindset applies whether you were creating a new product, rolling out a new software system, launching a global campaign, or seeking a new hire. It applies everywhere. In the event that you do not make your dates or you fall short of expectations, you need a solid contingency plan.

This instinctive rule applies in our daily transactions when consuming goods and services. If we buy something we no longer want, we fully expect to return it to a merchant and receive a refund, discount, or exchange. In the services world, we may receive an upgrade for lack of expected results.

Leadership is the ability to respond to uncertainty. The likelihood of change is always present; therefore, you need a team that can respond to that change. As a leader, how do you diffuse anxiety or unrest when there's a sudden change of course? While you cannot control future circumstances, you can speak to potential scenarios, instinctively planning for those potholes and your plan B.

> Early in Jessica's career, the following scene played over and over again: She would pitch an idea to her manager and then wait. Then she would wait some more—still waiting until something happened. One day in a meeting, someone else made that same pitch, which left her sunk in her chair thinking: "Hang on a minute, that was my idea, and someone else is now taking credit."

This scene replayed itself too many times until Jessica realized that the reason why she was not being listened to was because she wasn't positioning her ideas well enough. She had convinced herself that she wasn't being heard because she didn't contribute anything valuable to the team. In fact, she wasn't pitching anything. What she was doing was akin to taking a tiny piece of paper, scribbling some thoughts on it, slipping it under the door of her manager, and hoping that the manager would look down and see it someday.

How you do anything is how you do everything. If you aren't getting the visibility you deserve, are you taking responsibility for marketing yourself with an inspired enthusiasm that your clients can't ignore? If you have a low-key personality, you can pull this off by having the right attitude and good energy from being yourself. The biggest hurdle for leaders isn't in the design and development of ideas. The massive challenge is getting their products to market, and doing so with a quiet mention or as a casual message does not gain much traction.

Growing in leadership requires going against the grain and sticking your neck out consistently. In the end, it doesn't matter if your ideas are sold, although that's always the intention. What matters is that at the moment, you believe that you are valuable enough to open up to the room. The same mindset applies when you respectfully speak up and agree to disagree or need to ask the hard questions. Good leaders want to be challenged and challenge others to do the same. This means that you're doing your job well by growing a team of thinkers.

STRATEGIC THINKING

Many professionals seeking to grow as leaders share that they are concerned that their analytical skills could hinder their ability to think strategically. Leverage those analytical skills because they support your ability to instinctively choose the next best course of action. Professionals with strong analytical minds are able to creatively problem-solve, which is directly tied to effective decision making.

A powerful tool to support strategic thinking that results in the development of a broader vision is called *mind mapping*. Mind mapping is a thought process of walking through related ideas that create and reach a specific goal. It's an instinctive strategy that helps you flesh out the path to reaching an end state because it's based on how the human brain works. This map can chart a project, a goal, an initiative, or a problem that needs to be solved and follows the natural flow of how your brain processes information.

A mind map visually represents ideas and concepts that help structure and synthesize information to generate new ideas. Operating as a hub-and-spoke model, your brain takes one idea and branches out to another idea that forms a web of related thoughts that lead to a long-term vision. This is considered to be *critical thinking* and can be learned.

The benefit of mind mapping is that it not only helps you to get everything out of your head and onto paper but also helps you keep estimated resources and budgets front and center so that you don't fall prey to working in a vacuum. Replicating how your brain operates, you start with a central thought and branch out from there, letting it flow, so that the process can continuously unfold without filters or objections. You'll discover that the power of this approach lies in its simplicity.

When you first begin mind mapping, resist the urge to think serially. Keep going with it, and you will come to embrace it as a free-flowing stream of thought that will guide you in defining your multilayered strategy. Here's how to begin mind mapping:

- Start with the big-ticket ideas and concepts you should account for.
- Group them into individual categories.
- Continue to branch off from each one, with sublevel concepts falling underneath, forming a tree structure.

Write down your results as a first draft, and upon review, look for any blind spots around cost, time, and resources. When you provide a mind map, your colleagues can follow your reasoning, add to it, poke holes in it, and see if it still holds water. Run it by your colleagues to get their input so that you can circle back to address any problem areas before opening up your strategy to a wider audience. During formal discussions, you can later confidently handle those who raise their hands and ask, "Have you thought about X? Are we going to be covered then?" There is no need to be defensive or caught off guard in this situation because you are prepared to speak to those scenarios.

Other areas where leaders use mind mapping are where they seek to engage their team around a shared project vision and its breakdown into discrete workflows. Mind maps can also be used to align everyone with future goals, activities, and timelines. A mind map is also a great marketing tool to communicate with potential clients when you need to jump-start a conversation and make a great first impression. It demonstrates your thorough approach and creativity that delivers vital insight into how you think and what your team can bring to the table upon engagement, without you ever needing to say a word.

The Problem-Solution Map

Whereas some people perform better when they are under pressure from a single deadline, others find that stress steadily builds from being on the hook to produce. Whichever camp your team tends to fall into, when the alarm goes off, mind mapping will help your team move away from linear thinking and steadily engage in a collaborative process aimed at problem solving.

To create this problem-solution path, mind-map a realistic plan that will inspire your team to action. Aim for a short list of three potential solutions that will address the problem. As you walk through this problem-solution (P-S) map, assess the benefits and results of each proposed path. What costs are involved (i.e., do you need to pull in an external resource or extend the timeline?), and where does the group collectively rank on each solution? Is the potential path a stopgap measure that only meets a short-term goal, or is it sustainable in the long run? Do this for each possible result in your P-S map and step back, enabling the members of the team to recognize problems as opportunities for growth and empowering them to make a decision with consensus.

If you do not have all the information and data you need to develop a strategy, ask your clients to join your team and work backward. Ask questions to learn what your clients' priorities are, not what you feel is relevant. You may, for example, assume that you need months to learn a slice of a business area before you can dive into any planning, but that learning may not be directly related to the results your clients are actually seeking in the short term and could have you lose time.

When you take on a new leadership role, take a "help-me-to-help-you" position. You can be that human sponge, but don't feel compelled to have it all figured out on day one. This can quickly bury you in details and overwhelm you with the pressure to perform. Once these client conversations have begun, you can confidently step back and assess, map out a plan, and discover the key themes on which your team should focus. These then become the backbone of project plans that align teams.

You multiply your impact and value when others can leverage what you know—that's what thought leadership embodies. To be clear, though, not everyone knows what you know. You are growing each time you teach and share your knowledge so that others can take your tools and best practices and be successful. In turn, this further supports your own growth.

To avoid falling into perfection paralysis mode, know that not everyone will lead the same way as you. Take a deep breath on this one because under your leadership, your team members will follow their own instincts and improve your business function even further, which may likely look very different from how you've always approached it.

Good leaders teach their success principles and then let go, allowing their teams to grow. What are the expert areas that you know well that would enable others to achieve even better results? Don't get caught up in how you got to where you are in your career or compare yourself with others. Own it and allow others to make their own way.

Your success is driven by how willing you are to share your ideas and information, not from a scarcity mindset rooted in fear and the comfort of job security. Knowledge is power; yet still, there's no shortage of leaders who don't want to give up their power. The more power you share, the larger the impact and influence you have. To visualize this, look back to the people you knew in a position of power who kept all their knowledge to themselves instead of sharing it with others. Instinctive leadership is acting in spite of fear.

Leadership at times requires you to do the very thing that many people would not want to do for fear of disrupting an organization. While your job is not to be liked, you will get the support you need from others when you draw from the social capital you've established through marketing your own messaging.

A Rising Tide Lifts All Boats

As a purposeful leader, know that your rising tide comes from great people who together deliver exceptional performance, far greater than they could individually. You multiply your impact when you're willing to share your talents, skills, and experience to increase the overall performance of a cohesive unit rather than through a single contribution, which by its very nature will always be capped and never scale. Can you train 10 people? If you can train 10 people, can you also train 100 people? Leaders who influence not only market their message well but also multiply their results.

Unleash Your Power

Isabelle is a short and petite preteen. Given her height and skinny body frame, she could easily be perceived as a weak kid. In martial arts class, her sensei calls her out and asks her to demonstrate how to throw a fast, high, and hard kick to the class. Most of her peers are boys, older, and much taller than she is. Not quite sure why she was singled out, she rises, turns, and throws a high-flying kick at the target pad the instructor is holding. The instructor lifts the target pad higher, and Isabelle continues to ace it. Then she quietly returns to her spot and sits back down. She had never joined gymnastics or was particularly athletic when she was younger. Being extremely shy, she avoids any attention, and yet she instinctively stood up and performed upon command and demonstrated leadership by teaching others in the room.

No ego. No indecision or doubt. Answer the call, and give people your best results. You make your best decisions when, without hesitation, you instinctively take action. When you live life from a place of "let's see what happens," there's nothing to fear. You try it, and you see how you feel. If you like it, you do it again. If you don't, you may try something else. Effective leaders self-qualify to confidently express a vision of improving results without necessarily knowing every detail of how achieving those results will truly work in practice. Voice your ideas. Speak your vision. When exploring beyond what you currently know and are responsible for, you show your understanding of the bigger picture. Work backward and draw the end state; you can always circle back later on to color it all in.

Recognizing yourself as a thought leader is owning your reputation and your power to persuade—the ability to pull more people into your vision. Although it is a professional status that stands on its own, you will embrace thought leadership when it feels aligned with your purpose and helps you build warm and productive relationships. It establishes you as someone trustworthy in your industry and allows you to do more of the meaningful work you enjoy, and which makes a difference.

FEARLESSLY NETWORK

Build Your Professional Pipeline

In every belief where you feel you cannot be
successful at something, there is a counter belief
that intuitively knows it will make you grow.
Those impulses of thought are meant to fuel you to do
the one thing you fear the most so you can release it forever.

GO-GIVING, NOT GAINING

The basis of networking is often perceived to be ingenuine by nature. Emotionally, we do not feel good when we are selling ourselves strictly to gain versus give. You'll discover that your body's muscle response system proves this. Take any thought by which only you stand to benefit. For example, let's say that you criticize a peer instead of taking full responsibility for poor performance on a project. By doing so, you not only avoid admitting your mistake but also say something you know to be untrue. While you may have achieved a short-term win by saving your reputation, it could be overshadowed by feelings of regret. Acts such as this are shown to weaken the body based on diagnosis of the body's muscle response to certain events—as studied in the field of applied kinesiology. Muscle testing is thought to access our subconscious by delivering feedback from the body. It is based on the belief that when we experience mental stress, our muscles become weak without any awareness; the same applies when our thoughts harbor any feelings of self-doubt. Beliefs of strength and courage, however, through the use of words such as *I can* and *I am*, are shown to develop strong muscles and make us feel good because when saying them, we know them to be true. Feelings of appearing desperate when asking people to "keep us in mind," however, can physically weaken us; we may even find ourselves uncontrollably twitching from the discomfort alone. This goes against the grain of our emotional human makeup.

When you come from a place where only you stand to gain or are seeking a reward, such as a referral or free pass, you weaken yourself. However, when you come from a place of service, helping others or sharing something that can benefit them, you empower yourself.

The practice of generosity has been linked to a boost in happiness levels. When you give away some of your time or lend an ear to listen to someone with a desire to help, you feel a sense of abundance. In a study conducted at the University of Zurich, researchers showed scientific evidence that acts of generosity boost mood and mind, leading to greater happiness and "brain glow." A control group of 50 people were promised to receive various amounts of money. Some chose to spend the money on themselves while others planned to spend it on others. The area of the brain associated with altruism and happiness was consistently found to engage more intensely in those who chose to give the money to others. This group also reported higher levels of happiness after the study was over, not from the act of spending the money on others but from the *intention* to do so. If we practiced generosity as a consistent habit, it would ultimately lead to greater mental health and well-being. You'll also find increasing your network with more generous people will help move out any self-serving company you may have previously kept—those who tend to have an "I" versus "we" leadership approach.

When you are doing things for others, you feel good emotionally. Referring business to someone with no expectation of a return also feels good versus entering a room to join a pool of networkers shamelessly attempting to gain something, where everyone swimming around you is doing the same thing. Now imagine attending an evening networking event. This may not feel very inspiring. There you are, connecting with strangers mindlessly, stirring a straw in a cocktail glass, having empty conversations. Where do you start? How do you walk away knowing that having invested two hours of your time is time well spent?

> Ripe opportunities typically come from those who have not worked with you or know you very well and yet remember how they felt around you, therefore referring you on.

If, in your role, you have typically worked behind the scenes, say in research or engineering, you likely would feel out of your comfort zone in networking because of the very nature of your work, which requires little collaboration and human exchange. Dealing out business cards isn't exactly your natural state of being. It requires casual conversation and some level of navigating the art of small talk—finding topics of common interest to discuss with strangers so that you can build ongoing relationships that may turn out to be fruitful later on. Who knows? It's a hit or miss. You also may not have ever needed to flex a networking muscle in your entire life, so doing that now can feel daunting.

If you have been grounded mainly in the technical or functional aspects of your role, then networking is a great way to get advice from those in other business areas you otherwise would not have access to. This can be just the feedback you need to determine how you can grow further in leadership at your organization or elsewhere.

Many professionals admit that while they have no problem meeting new people, they still tend to shy away from networking on the first introduction. Engaging in casual chitchat and making small talk can stir an innate fear of looking foolish if you don't know how to position yourself on introduction. Walking into a room filled with ideal contacts who can refer you on, only to stammer upon any introduction and walk away empty-handed, can also set your confidence back significantly. You will quickly recognize a lack of clarity when you are unable to convey to someone what you actually do in your career and, more important, what you are looking for. You may ask yourself, "Why am I here?" Granted, this can be disappointing, but consider this experience well worth the effort. You will learn a lot from observing what you did not say so that you can focus on what you can say the next time around.

Merely hearing your own words and where they fall flat will tell you whether you are doing a good job of representing yourself. Answering the question "So, what do you do?" that first time can feel like a squeaky wheel. Many professionals in this type of setting can feel their self-esteem drop so low that they vow to never put themselves in that public situation again, just from hearing how weak and unclear they sounded.

Build Your Professional Pipeline Before You Need It

If you have ever stepped into a sales leadership role, your pipeline is the key element and driver of your marketing and professional success. A pipeline is what holds a sales leader's book of business, which is a list of potential clients that you have engaged with over time and will likely convert from prospects to paying customers. Much like any successful rainmaker, you too are in the marketing business. You are always selling yourself by developing your pipeline of people who will refer you, advocate for you, and put their name on the line by passing your name on to someone they trust.

Your pipeline also includes people with whom you can partner, either internally or externally, who will freely share their best career advice with you and introduce you to new opportunities when the occasion presents itself. In the spirit of reciprocity, your pipeline is where personal and professional partnerships are made.

Rationally, we understand that networking is *the* high-touch factor needed to find opportunities, resources, and insights in our careers. Yet connecting with people who can potentially help us grow or share unpublished information that we should keep an eye on based on the company rumor mill is still met with resistance. Don't be put off by this must-have rite of passage in business. Whittled down, it's no more than relationship building that helps you turn on your radar for opportunities you are leaving on the table. Successful leaders don't build hit-and-run relationships; they form bonds with other professionals that can last a lifetime and on which they can rely as a mutual support system.

If you're going to invest your time cultivating a professional pipeline and make it work for you, keep in mind that people do not give referrals or do business with people they do not trust. Whenever you're in need of a plumber or an electrician, you are likely to reach out to friends and neighbors as a trusted referral resource. This same mindset applies to your career.

Giving away referrals to support others who trust you, while equally important, should be handled delicately. If a close friend asks you to refer him or her for a just-published opportunity at your workplace and you knew that that person has a track record of being a flight risk at previous jobs, for example, leaving after just six months in, would you put your name on the line to support that person? You may deeply appreciate your relationship, but the person's predictable poor job performance puts you at risk because your reputation is now attached to his or her name. You may not choose to stick your neck out so swiftly if it means compromising the trust others have in you. Although your intention may be to support someone, listen carefully to your instincts when you feel an introduction could place a trusted relationship you have developed now at risk.

MAKE YOURSELF MEMORABLE

Your closest circle of friends occupies the same universe as you.
People outside your immediate sphere are likely
to have contact with different people and hear about
career opportunities that you wouldn't otherwise hear of.[1]

Fearless networking is where you effectively build relationships among industry colleagues and peers. Unfortunately, there's a harsh perception that you need to resort to "in-your-face" methods to do this well, which can lower your energy to a point where you no longer feel confident. Not so. You can find your "in" and engage with anyone in any formal or casual conversation so that others will want to learn more about you. It should be an inviting space for you to share who you are and why you're there. Although your knee-jerk outreach would be to rely on close friends and family to support you in your career, the reality is that your next opportunity likely will come from loose, casual connections and acquaintances. The likelihood of your close ties helping you fan out your wider network is lower because you share the same circles. Networking leverages the power of many.

Granted, there is peace and predictability when you are at rest, keeping to your normal course of action. You have control over your immediate environment. Stepping out of your silo, however, by making connections is statistically proved to increase your chances for opportunity through the simple act of sending a clear message: "This is who I am. This is how I've led. This is what I am capable of producing in my career. This is what I'm looking for. Can you help?"

On the surface, this process may seem mundane; yet energetically, it will give you clarity on how well you have positioned yourself simply by allowing you to notice how you feel when you hear your own voice and see others' reaction to you. Did your message land well, and was it clear enough?

It's normal to feel uncomfortable when you put yourself out there, not knowing what to say. You may return home feeling defeated by the experience. Since childhood, our characters were formed based on how comfortable we were openly sharing of ourselves with others. If you feel some resistance toward self-expression, consider how well you feel understood by others today. When you initially feel out of place in networking, ill-prepared, and not clear on what you are genuinely looking for, it can feel like you've taken two steps back. This is a distorted place your ego will attempt to bury you in if you allow it. Consider this seeming setback an instinctual nudge to shift into focus. Your awareness of not having clarity on how to advocate for yourself is the wake-up call.

Owning your authority is engaging in self-reflection and allowing yourself to learn from every setback. When you see a look of confusion when you introduce yourself, let that be your signal—your message was too broad or unclear. You need to reel it in and tweak and pinpoint an area that speaks to you and what you deliver.

Be good to yourself. Honor that cloudy space and consider what you want your message to be. This will help you to speak up with crystal clarity. Energetically, you will also feel your body make a positive shift that will raise your confidence level.

Pick an area where you are comfortably confident in your career and talk about the results you deliver. I worked with data for over two decades, but I didn't introduce myself by saying I was managing a global data management shop. Instead, I'd say, "I help companies make strategic decisions based on the data analytics my team delivers." Start with your end product and work backward; the words will come, and if they don't feel right, you can tweak your pitch, refining it further until it becomes sharp enough to cut through the noise and any confusion.

If you work in compliance, for example, you keep your organization out of trouble by keeping an eye on new regulations and identifying potential risk. Protecting your company from harm, both legally and ethically, is what you do and easy enough for someone not familiar with that field to understand.

MARKET YOUR MESSAGE

Whenever you seek to make a career transition, the reality is that you'll never put that desire in motion until you begin sharing it. Your intention must go beyond sitting behind your phone and computer. Owning your authority is putting yourself inside conversations that require you to talk about what you do as if you are already in that new role. When you feel qualified in your mind to show up with that kind of energy, that's when you can keep it authentically you, unattached to what anyone thinks of you. You have locked in how you want to be perceived.

Networking is a powerful sounding board to discover what your potential is. You'll get instant feedback if, on sharing what you do for a living, you see eyes glazing over. Your gut will tell you to swiftly change course. When you make yourself visible through networking, the process works as a simple filtration system. Speaking up about yourself as a professional expert must feel genuine. Anything you say that doesn't flow effortlessly must be refined further. This can also mean facing negative self-talk such as:

"I will not be taken seriously."

"I will look foolish."

"I am not qualified."

Do you hear any fears showing up? There's the current role you have been in for X number of years, and then there's the new role you want to be in. Therefore, you want to talk about that new position as if you already have it.

There are only three things that you have any control of: your beliefs (which are just thoughts that have become locked in as truth), your actions (your behavior), and your images of the future and whether those images are positive or negative. Your thoughts are energy that others can feel, so even if you are not entirely confident when you first start to network, you must talk about your next career move from a place of feeling qualified and as if you already are there. This is how you will find your next opportunity, including meeting those who may already be in that line of work.

Professionals who consider exiting their corporate jobs to work for themselves often struggle with their messaging as they get their business off the ground. Yet once they speak of their work with passionate enthusiasm, they will feel themselves relax. It feels so much more authentic when you own your authority, speaking of what you are expert in. Knowing that you have the potential to pivot in a new direction by sharing your knowledge, you can own it.

You continue to refine your marketing message over time, showcasing your value. Eventually, it no longer feels like networking. It's a sounding board to perfect a sales message that you otherwise would never craft had you not fearlessly networked. You are in the marketing business. What do you uniquely deliver that others need, and how can they begin working with you? When you bring this kind of clear, intentional energy, you can let go in full faith that your time invested in building relationships will attract the resources and opportunities you need when you need them. When you have that kind of clarity, those who meet you are clear as well.

Build Your Street Credibility

Today, how plugged in you are in business comes shining through from the number of LinkedIn connections you have. It's a widely accepted measure of your level of credibility and influence. The more people with whom you are connected both online and offline, the more opportunities you will have to reach out and explore a potential relationship. Consistently building your professional pipeline results in a trusted referral network on which you can rely for years to come.

If you consider yourself more of a low-key, mindful professional, you may not be the social butterfly who will politely touch down to collect business cards. You may prefer standing at the perimeter of a room to observe people filing in. You may want to "feel the room" before you "work the room" to feel safe. When you listen to your gut, you will always instinctively know in what direction to walk; the person you suddenly choose to sit next to at a table is not random.

There is a fundamental human need to feel safe before we speak, which is why we carefully observe how we fit in before stepping into a new situation. Intuitively, our antennas are raised to full height, guiding us on whom we should migrate toward at the hors d'oeuvre table. This then begets the question, when you walk into a room full of strangers, what would create an ideal safe space for you to speak naturally?

Consider a situation in which you are in a room of networkers, and all the people who approach you want to know what kind of referral you are looking for, eagerly wanting to know what brought you to the event and how they can help. This would exponentially help you cut to the chase, remove any unnecessary schmoozing, and eliminate time circling the room. These lovely strangers would make it super easy for you to focus and ask for what you want. A match made in networking heaven could easily be made. No discomfort. No fear. No negative images or disappointment.

If you tend to be more reserved in public situations, what if you instead flip this scenario around and do that for others, introducing yourself and asking, "What kind of referral are you looking for? What brings you to this event? Maybe I am someone who can help."

Here you are working what's called the *law of reciprocity*, where the more you give to others, the more you can expect to receive. Psychologists explain the reasoning behind this law and why it works as a natural impulse: when someone does something good for you, you have a deep-rooted desire to reciprocate and do something good for that person in exchange. The next time you meet someone, make the first move generously. Be curious about others; the conversation will inevitably always come right around to you and what you are looking for.

A great conversation starter is to observe something that you admire about someone. This can be a piece of jewelry the person is wearing or a new tech gadget the person is holding. You can talk about the conference or event itself or even trade opinions on the keynote content. You can ask a question or the person's opinion on the speaker. Then, simply listen generously to what others need. Give them your card if you can help. If not, gracefully exit the conversation and move on. This keeps it short and sweet and saves you much precious time. Finding quality contacts will support you more than how many hands you shake.

Also, pay close attention to the first thing people talk about when they first introduce themselves. Whatever comes up from their gut at first blush is what they are likely most proud of in their career. This will help you easily focus and be present when you listen to what brings them pride. The benefit of this technique is that it will put you at ease and allow you easily to know what you should say next. We can readily become anxious sitting in the spotlight when the conversation turns around to us. Being a good listener, however, is still staying active in a conversation and can allay any uneasiness. Through direct eye contact and body movement that leans in, people can feel when they have someone's attention and the person is tuning in.

Be mindful of your time when you place yourself in networking events; you are there to create relationships the same as everyone else, and yet chattiness can be your Achilles' heel in social situations. A ripe connection can be made in less than five minutes. One or two quality connections are all you need to make an evening end productively with time well spent.

Be Intentional

When you are dining at a restaurant and you place your order, there is never any doubt about receiving the meal you asked for or any emotion attached to your preference. Whatever your choice, it just *is*. Bring that same energy of intention to networking. Do you want:

- An introduction to someone?
- To hear of new trends and insights in your area of the business?
- Advice on how to handle a challenging aspect of your work?
- A new job or key contact at a particular organization?

Just as important is internal networking inside your organization, which often requires building trust between people in your business area and those in other groups. Your intention as a business leader may be to build back a relationship that strategically positions your team at the forefront, leading as the number one service provider of another side of an organization.

Be aware of any feelings coming up when you consider what your intention is. Be present to any limiting beliefs that surface as though you are a third party. You can, for example, be inheriting a group that has built a reputation of underperformance, and your intention may be to win back recognition for the group members as exemplary performers. Sweep aside any concerns that place you in a weakened position through association by becoming an observer of that negative thought process and questioning whether those limiting beliefs are true. What do your instincts say?

Go back to your intention. What do you want? How would you know that you have found a ripe opportunity or contact if you're not clear on what you want? Saying you want a new leadership opportunity somewhere else isn't enough. Maybe you want to meet someone who is in a similar role but in a different industry. Partnering with a counterpart to pick that person's brain could spawn a melting pot of creative ideas for each of you. Maybe you are following an organization you want to work for, so gaining an introduction from someone who works there would be a great first step.

Possibly you are like I was when I was in my twenties. I felt sheltered from being in one position after a year or two. I felt that I should get out more and listen to what other professionals were doing in my industry. A specific intention that I had was to meet more women leaders in technology, because at the time, there were no female role models in tech on Wall Street.

Without a clear intention, you will end up with a pocketful of soon-to-be stale business cards. The same applies to meetings. Owning your authority is asking, "What is it that I want to walk away with?"

This then creates opportunities so that the people you connect with are aligned with that intention. Nothing is ever random. The people you meet may very well be able to support you directly or point you to someone who can help.

This may seem obvious. Shouldn't you always know what you want? *Yes* and *no*. What you want needs to be specific enough so that your brain, the creative goal-seeking organism that it is, will find the people, resources, and opportunities it needs. Treat this like a game, because, on some level, that's what it is. It can be as simple as, "I am kicking back today with self-care" or "I am connecting with someone who can refer me on to a great job opportunity." This is dialing in your intention so that you can focus on what you want. You are guaranteed to create your desired experience because your brain is now wired to find what it's looking for.

Ever notice when you are in the market to buy a new car, say you have a desire for a red Jeep, that suddenly as you are driving to work, you see the exact make and model of the car you want? Red Jeeps are everywhere. Your subconscious is very selective in what it gives its attention to when you become intentional about what you want. Your brain takes the flood of information you're giving it all day every day and focuses in on a single image based on the thoughts that are uppermost in your mind. In truth, there hasn't been an actual influx of red Jeeps suddenly; you are just intentionally homing in on what you want to experience.

Dress for success! Lead with a curious and generous attitude. This is another strategy that you can bring to your next meet-up to create a worthwhile and productive experience. Use the following approaches:

- Wear an accessory that makes you feel good and/or makes you memorable—a fun, colorful tie, a unique brooch, a sophisticated pair of cufflinks that exude confidence.
- Wear a color that raises your energy level and makes you feel good—your power color.
- Wear a smart pair of comfortable shoes to feel at ease.

Although, like many, you may not be a fan of the business card, let's recognize its value. There's only one reason why you would want to take one from someone when you first meet—to connect and reconnect, keeping the person inside your professional pipeline. Be sure to email the person or connect on LinkedIn soon after, while your encounter is still memorable. Once you are connected with people, they will catch any news or activity buzzing around you online. Any activity feed you share on social media is kept continuously on their radar.

Email also gives you the opportunity to drop a quick line, re-introduce yourself, and simply "keep them in mind" should you hear of anything that could support them and vice versa.

The purpose of marketing (and networking, for that matter) is to do one thing—to remain on people's minds, to be on their radar. Your goal is to connect before they forget you and to keep those relationships simmering. This can be done by sharing an article that pertains to your industry or a white paper as a resource.

You are in the relationship business. If you write a blog, you don't have readers; you have relationships. If you run a podcast, you don't have listeners; you have relationships. Even if you just send a weekly status report that reaches your organization's leaders, you have readers who subscribe to you. Be on the minds of those who are ready to hire you or refer you on. Get creative about ways to maintain like-minded relationships and ripe connections with people, and when it feels right, from your gut, ask them for a direct connection.

Select Your Centers of Influence

You can pinpoint centers of influence in a heartbeat. These are professionals who know a lot of other people; they thrive on connecting people together and are better known as social butterflies of the business world. They are very essential contacts, and there is no doubt that you know at least one such person today who can support you right now.

You can approach a person who is a center of influence to simply pick his or her brain. There's a ton of value in listening to how such a person approaches business and how that person has shaped his or her career. You can also choose a person of influence who can create an "in" for you in the industry, at a specific company, or in a role in which you are interested, sharing not-yet-published opportunities, news, or events.

If at a pure networking event or in a relationship where you have established some rapport, feel free to ask, "Who do you know who . . . [insert ideal contact for whom you are searching]?" For example, "Who do you know who works in the asset management area at this investment bank?" or "Who do you know who works in business development in the manufacturing industry?"

Be open, approach the unapproachable, and when you meet a person of influence, never walk away without obtaining his or her contact information. Such people will usually offer the best way to get in touch with them anyway and tell you to "reach out any time," but be sure to ask.

If you don't have access to a person who is a center of influence, there are many ways to seek such people out. You can join groups they belong to on LinkedIn. You can use these groups as your sounding board, to ask a question, or to seek advice. You can ask friends which people of influence they may know and ask for an introduction. You can extend your manager's presence by introducing yourself to his or her business partners while speaking on your manager's behalf. Listen closely to any questions or issues they wish to address, and assure them that you will "take that back" to your boss, positioning yourself as a center of influence while building a "go-giver" relationship at the same time. Lean into creative ways you can become a powerful "bridger" yourself, where you can serve as a center of influence for others as well as increase your influence, establish yourself further, and fan out your network. Inside organizations, there is usually no doubt who the centers of influence are. You can meet them at internal networking events or at the tail end of meetings as you're exiting a conference room.

GREETING, NOT MEETING

Have you ever subconsciously written off a contact because he or she is off limits? Be aware of the people you may be filtering out because you have heard their reputation possibly put in a negative light:

"He's a workaholic."

"His door is always closed, and he is unapproachable."

"She's a perfectionist and expects everyone around her to be as well."

Let's assume for a moment that the rumor mill is true. If so, use this to your advantage. What better way to feed someone's ego than to reach out for the person's words of wisdom and guidance? Turn away from the noise, and go with your gut, leading with intention. Don't fall prey to assumptions based on textbook gossip. Fall back to your instincts. Your relationship with such a person can look entirely different from someone else's experience. This stigma could apply to you as well should you be inheriting a role that has long held to a reputation of poor performance.

If nothing comes of a connection and you never hear back (it happens), reassess. Nothing lost, nothing gained. Therefore, it's a wash—but you still took on some risk. There is much to be gained when you treat professional networking as a numbers game. You exercise a dormant muscle you may have never known you had. You get much better at asking for opportunities and referrals when you are detached from the outcome yet still remain intentional. It's when you get so caught up in how things should pan out that you get frustrated when it doesn't go your way and, in turn, you give up. You set yourself up for failure, feeling let down and convinced that you are not good enough when, in reality, you simply have to be clear on what you want and let the rest work itself out. Impatience can be your downfall. When you show up with positive expectations, you set up your environment with fertile ground in which to plant the seeds that will reap the fruits of your labor later on.

Pride is another factor at play. When you network or take the "Who do you know who . . . ?" approach, you believe that you are bothering people by merely asking for their time to keep you in mind. Here's a quick strategy to use if you have any hesitation about walking into a "cold" room to build lasting professional connections: Pretend that it's your party. Assume that you called everyone together that evening and that they are all there, in that room, to meet none other than *you*. As their host, you are weaving in and out of small-group circles to see who has arrived. If you were indeed the one who organized the event and invited everyone into your home, how would that change how you show up? How would that change how you are perceived when you clearly state what you do and how they (your guests) could help you? It's natural to think, "I want the right person's name and number. I want a new job opportunity." Do you hear how instead of making it about the people you meet, you are making it all about *you* in there?

Mindset shift: While everyone may be there to see you, it's not about you. It's about how you make people feel. How included they feel in the room. Once you flip that limiting belief around and recognize that your job is to make people feel safe and in good hands on your watch, you earn their trust and attention. Likewise, you need to feel safe as well. Treat others as you would want to be treated if the tables were turned. Your job as a host would be to make sure that your guests' drinks are filled, learn what they are looking for, discover how you can help, and listen generously.

To get what you need, you have to consider the wants and needs of your guests because they are thinking the same thing. Position yourself to ask by learning what's in it for them, not just you. The conversation inevitably will turn right back around in your direction anyway, and your guests will ask how they can support you as well and ask, "Who is an ideal connection that you're looking for?"

BIRDS OF A FEATHER FLOCK TOGETHER

Aside from strictly in-person connections, you can also tap into building your network online as well. Over a decade ago, I posted a leadership event I wanted to hold in London on LinkedIn as a hypothetical. I submitted it inside a UK group. It is important to note that this was back when LinkedIn was not the buzzing online business hub it is now. I was very clear about what I wanted to deliver at this event, what city I wanted to hold it in, and what I needed to make it happen. At the tail end of that post and as more of a postscript, I was fully transparent and mentioned that I would need a company or organization to host me. Making myself somewhat vulnerable, I shared that I didn't know anyone in London and put that small but essential detail front and center, allowing the energy I put out there to do its thing. A few days later, I was contacted by an international law firm headquartered in London. Not only did the company want to sponsor my event for its female lawyers and their clients, but it also opened the event up to the public as well. Location secured, the event occurred at full capacity in the heart of London, facing a gorgeous view of the River Thames. This was more than I could have imagined. My time and energy investment were nominal. It took me less than five minutes to share that post and ask my question. It was a gutsy move to throw an event out across the Atlantic and act as-if. Today, I am still in regular contact with those who attended that event and the people they have since introduced me to, strengthening our mutual networks. Following your instincts is acting as-if.

Nothing Happens Without a Commitment

When you are on the cusp of creating something great in your life, you will find more reasons to stay put and dry from the rain, play it safe, and remain warm inside. What you may find, however, is that by pushing against those impediments, you will see doors fly open, encouraging you to keep going. Note the order of operations here. Doors don't fly open until you've put some skin in the game and made the commitment first. When you are clear and determined on what you want to create, that's when you summon a force field of momentum and resilience. You wave away the furiously blinking stop signs from your ego warning you to "Watch out! Dangerous territory ahead! You're not ready! Do you really think you can pull this off? Who do you think you are?"

You cannot steer a parked car. You silence the ego when you calmly acknowledge its presence right next to you in the passenger seat. Hit the gas and drive in the direction you desire despite your uninvited guest.

Look for events in your industry that attract your ideal contacts and where they would typically hang out. Remember, a ripe connection is someone who knows a lot of people and who can potentially help you. Industry events and intimate executive dinners functioning as roundtables are often found on conference websites; so, for example, if you are in finance living in [insert local city], simply search for "finance conference [insert local city]." Virtual hangouts online are just as common as live and in-person ones.

When I was working in Financial Services, I would sign up for small and intimate industry dinners with technology leaders, where the dinners would beheld in roundtable format. These dinners were complimentary because the hosting organization would gather industry experts to further their brand. By pulling in professionals in major city hubs, these hosting organizations positioned themselves as leaders of influence in their industry. In such venues, you have the opportunity to create quality elbow-to-elbow relationships, given the small-group format, that can pay off for a lifetime.

Cast Your Line: Donate Your Time

One of the best ways to creatively market yourself through networking is to get involved in service opportunities, where you donate your time with a social element. Sign yourself up to cook in a soup kitchen, plant a community garden, or build a home in a low-income community.

Participating in "Take your child to work" day was an ideal opportunity that I participated in early in my career, and it increased my internal network significantly at my organization. I volunteered to teach a one-hour computer programming class to our little visitors each year. I brought the same energy and professionalism I would if I were presenting to a board of directors. I created a welcome packet for my students, who enthusiastically took their seats at the long boardroom table with their laptops flipped open. I taught a lesson plan, took questions, led step-by-step exercises, and overall had a fantastic time go-giving. Ironically, these were my pre-parenting years when having children was not yet a goal of mine. Instinctively, one year in, I decided to put my business card in the take-home goody bags to make myself memorable. In a single lunch hour, I was given the eyeballs of senior executives who looked on gratefully from the back of the room as I taught their curious children something new and valuable. Make no mistake; these weren't just parents. They were influencers with whom I could easily socialize for years to come. I self-created a platform to introduce who I was and what kind of work I did at the company before training began. From then on, whenever I walked into the company kitchen or other social setting, Christmas party, or employee going-away soirees, I was making cozy chitchat and small talk with leaders I would have otherwise never connected with. By giving away my time, I was able to get my name out there quickly, establishing trusted relationships that would last for years and increase my own influence as a business leader in my industry.

What are some ways that you can create an in with people who can support you in your career? Volunteering is an ideal opportunity because you have direct access to connect while being of service, doing something that you enjoy. These situations also remove any fear that you may normally have about approaching others. If it speaks to you, consider this another networking strategy that clears the path for you to feel good about handing out your business card and furthering a relationship. There are also external company events that foster relationship-building, from local nonprofits to offsite workplace celebrations.

Consider how you can build authentic camaraderie with others at professional events? You can, for example:

- Sit on a career panel.
- Join a board of directors or steering committee.
- Participate in a mentoring event.
- Catch up with college alumni.
- Be interviewed on a stage for your leadership advice.

There are endless possibilities on how you can connect to reconnect later. Treat your business relationships as you would any friendship in which you haven't seen each other for decades. That friendship can be reignited years later or kept warm so that you feel genuine whenever you do reach out. There is no rule book or statute of limitations on the number of years you must maintain a relationship before reaching out. The good news is while people may not always remember what you do for a living, they will never forget how you made them feel.

Speak on Their Stage

Stretching yourself further, what types of venues can you attend as a featured speaker? Being a speaker is the most effective one-to-many approach to raising your credibility and influence in order to gain visibility in your industry quickly. As a speaker or panel participant, you aren't working the floor meeting people on a one-on-one basis any longer. You can highlight what you do and deliver advice to substantiate yourself as a subject matter expert to hundreds of people at one time.

When I began getting invitations to speak at information technology (IT) roundtables and conferences, I intuitively felt that I was being pulled into the future I wanted as a technology leader. I didn't know what would come around the corner, and I didn't care. I thought, "Well, if I'm still the trusted technologist who is being invited to be her own publicist by owning her value, I'd better still accept those speaking invitations."

This was an impulse that felt aligned with my career goals, so I accepted every speaking invitation. This never felt icky and uncomfortable to me because I gave away a ton of content, sharing my lessons learned, answering questions, delivering value in exchange for the right to self-promote, and furthering my brand inside my field in front of an audience of leaders across industries, all while remaining authentic to who I was.

I share this for one reason. If there are organizations with which you have become involved, then leverage that opportunity using your subject area of knowledge to speak on their stages. Successful leaders keep their opportunistic eyes wide open. They share their ideas with larger audiences while establishing themselves as experts, and qualifying themselves to share what they know and learned to get to where they are. In terms of time, it takes less than a week to find either a speaking opportunity or any online or offline platform where you can present either inside your industry or across industries.

There are people out there who can learn from you and who don't know what you know. There are things that you do in your sleep that you are taking for granted because you do them so well. Don't underestimate the doors that will fly open even years later from the simple act of being of service in this way. I had multiple job offers that were often sourced from these kinds of speaking gigs and fully acknowledged how I created them. I wasn't a rock star. I kept my ego in check. I was leading others with what I knew and what I felt proud and passionate talking about. If there are people who feel they will benefit from what you have to say, then your job is half done. The only thing left is to "edutain" your listeners. Educate and entertain with personal storytelling (which I'll cover in more detail in Chapter 5). These are excellent and often overlooked opportunities to increase your influence.

Brown bag lunches are excellent informal meetings often thrown together so that one expert from an organization can be invited to do one thing—share what he or she knows. At my organization, when we held these lunches, everyone from technology, finance, trading, and compliance would eat, listen, and learn. The designated host and business leader would talk about his or her corner of the world in the organization and, more important, how his or her area contributed to the bigger picture of the company's results. These lunches not only served as great social events for employees; they also were educational, and attendees always walked away with a broader understanding of how the company ran. These events are ripe opportunities for you to be that leader of influence as well. No planning, no agenda; we often pulled people from overseas offices (these were virtual as much as they were in person). You can simply nominate someone every month and shout it out over a calendar invite so that everyone has an opportunity to attend. If you are genuinely interested in others and their interests, you also encourage them to open up and share a little of themselves with the room, further growing an inclusive culture.

If these strategies feel like too much of a stretch, great news—you are right where you need to be. Let those code red stop signs coming from your ego become your instinctual triggers instead. I'd like to remind you of the risk that comes from doing things as you have always done them. Operating in a vacuum in one corner of a business, quietly churning out good work without casting out your line to others who may need support or, worse, not knowing what kind of support they need, works both ways. In turn, you are not considered a valuable resource for others. You are not on anyone's radar. You are walking away from opportunities on the table that you would otherwise have had access to, which later can feel like an isolated place to be.

This is a choice you make each day: step into the unknown while fully intending a positive outcome that is no different from when you set a thermostat to feel more comfortable in a room. This is more than just knowing and doing the things you need in your career. It's being inside conversations and relishing human connection. It's being self-aware by knowing who you are and trusting that the connections you build and maintain are aligned purposefully and therefore become a solid future investment. Why else would you allocate your most precious resource—time—unless you understand what's in it for you?

Looking at the areas in your life that have had the least growth, ask yourself what is one thing you can do that will move you from a state of powerlessness to one where you have free rein. Your internal dialogue and gut instinct can bring back your power to choose. If you were about to lead a presentation and you said to yourself, "I will flop and make a fool of myself," energetically, this self-talk has already projected a negative outcome, which, in turn, creates a negative feeling in your body and weak muscles that others will feel even if you don't miss a beat and pull off your presentation brilliantly.

Owning your power is feeling your way into what's intuitively good for you. You will never be perceived as quiet or weak when you make it a nonnegotiable to lead intentionally when you enter any given situation, networking or otherwise. Embrace your need to listen and process, and trust what's next for you. This inside-out approach self-qualifies you to meet opportunities when they arise, find your voice, and own your authority in time every time.

Look Up and Across the Ladder

If you were ready to buy a new car, it's safe to say that you would go for a test drive before making such a large investment. Why not apply the same mindset to your career? When people share that they want to pivot in a new career direction, my first question always is, "Have you done the test drive? Have you reached out to those who are already in that role? If you don't ask, how will you know if you will like it?"

This approach applies whether you wish to stay at your organization or explore opportunities elsewhere to advance in leadership. Seek out those who have been in those shoes—in that desired role. Retirees, for example, would welcome the opportunity to be asked to share their true stories from a successful career. Hunt for them, find them, and learn all that you can from them so that you have enough data to make a sound career transition. By simply asking the question and identifying your ideal role models who can offer practical inside career advice, you've already set in motion the likelihood that you will find them.

Your mind will work night and day to focus on that intention, and your instincts will guide you successfully.

Nurturing a professional pipeline can also help you find the right contacts who can serve as sounding boards with whom to share ideas, especially if they are leading similar business areas. Follow your gut on where you can best locate a counterpart with your same role sitting inside another organization or industry and see how he or she is handling challenges that are similar to yours. You can take that knowledge back to your shop and team. You can find these external advisors at industry conferences, through business partners or third parties with whom you are working, or upon asking for an introduction. Networking with diverse professionals in your industry or on forums allows people to learn from one another as much as well as provides ripe opportunities to connect and build relationships.

This approach requires leaving your comfort zone, asking what questions you should be asking and don't yet know, and learning from others' failures as much as from their successes. Consider the professional pipeline in your own organization and key insiders you can lean on as advisors. Which of them have already reached your desired level of leadership? Have you ever asked how they did it? Don't sit on ceremony; ask for their advice. Pick their brains. Be unattached to the answer; make yourself vulnerable. Keep an ear out for how others have developed their careers in-house, navigating the system, and have grown their influence. Building your internal network and community of advocates, you will find, becomes just as critical to your success.

YES! ASK AND EXPECT IT EVERY TIME

*Is what you are doing today moving you closer
to where you want to be tomorrow?*

ASKING IS A MUSCLE

If you were to measure how often you have *asked* in your career—asking for more budget or resources, asking for a project commitment, asking for clarity before making a key decision, or asking for more time so that you or your team can ramp up with additional training—on a scale of one to ten, where would you say that you fall? This is a performance metric that you want to keep a close eye on, because if your score falls anywhere below five, you are not maximizing your potential and you are leaving valuable opportunities on the table.

If you notice a pattern where the *yeses* are not flooding in, you are either not advocating for yourself enough or not asking the right questions of others. Simply asking for help is a powerful tool that you can employ strategically; yet it is often avoided because of a fear of rejection and of being judged negatively.

Fear will always crop up, but when you recognize it and call it out as if it is sitting right next to you in the room, that's when you can ask for what you want in spite of fear. When you work your ability to ask for things consistently, you raise your confidence level by becoming desensitized to the outcome, and therefore, you become much better at advocating for yourself. This process of letting go with detached expectation becomes so significant that you'll find that you have greater ease when managing conflict and that you even welcome performance feedback upon request.

If you consider yourself to be more on the passive side, then you are less likely to ask for resources that can support you, which has both a payoff and a price tag. The payoff can be the "I'll do it myself" mentality, where you satisfy a need to be in control by accomplishing everything on your own as opposed to delegating and trusting others to make decisions. This need for control of your environment can also show up on projects that depend on another division's deliverables yet have a direct impact on your own results. It is sometimes easier to roll up your sleeves and get the job done yourself rather than take the time to train a team or to ask for help or for someone to step up and take responsibility when needed. The cost, in contrast, is always your time and possibly creating a chokehold on projects, painting yourself in a corner, or missing opportunities to be tapped to lead more strategic initiatives. The members of your team would also perceive a lack of trust and a lack of investment in them to achieve the same results, fostering a culture of unattainable perfectionism.

You can see the significance of asking when you work out the division of labor at home as well. You may negotiate whose turn it is to take out the garbage, fold the laundry, cook dinner, or do the food shopping each week. You are constantly faced with decisions on who does what and when. When one partner takes on less responsibility, resentment can quickly creep in. You may both later fall into a routine and eventually work out a system as a family, but this process only comes from asking.

The same applies to your career. There are endless opportunities on the table that you may be filtering out. When you embrace your fears for what they are—usually self-created negative images of the future—and act anyway, that's when you are instinctively led to ask for what you want, including choosing the right people to reach out to and rely on.

This is a numbers game. The more people you ask, the more likely it is that you will find someone to support you. There is so much power and confidence in this approach—allow it to build your momentum, and keep asking, irrespective of any outcome.

Studies show that the success rate of sales professionals closing their deals is 93 percent, and all the closings are made on the sixth client phone call. Keeping this statistic in mind, it stands to reason that if you expect to eventually receive the outcomes you want, you want to be persistent with the follow-up.

Radio Silence Is Not *No*

One of the biggest mistakes that stop people from asking is the assumption that radio silence means *no*. Years ago, I received a piece of feedback from a client that changed the game for me professionally and that I have never forgotten. My client said, "We always appreciated your persistence because you were never pushy about it." Every *no* brings you closer to a *yes*.

Consider all the things you want in your life. These can relate to your finances, health, career, or relationships. If I told you that you can have whatever you want in those areas but that you have to ask for them regularly until you receive the results you want, would you still ask?

Now assume that the *yes* is given when you ask for anything across those areas. Leaning into your gut, what shows up as a natural next step? Instinctively, you may pick up the phone, write an email, leave a note for someone on his or her desk, or take someone out to lunch. The law of probability states that the more times you experiment with something, the closer you get to a probable outcome. You can begin working this law right now by asking three to five people daily until you achieve any goal you want. Often what you experiment with is driven by instinct, choosing the right time or feeling enough positive energy in a room to be able to "ride the wave" to build momentum, influencing morale.

No matter the target, your brain, as the goal-seeking organism that it is, will work overtime to make your goal happen. Your intuition will consistently guide you in finding the resources you need and the people you should call. You learn to trust your instinct over time, even if, for example, four of five people you contact don't lead anywhere meaningful. If you hear or feel the words *no* or *not right now*, visualize your *yes* even stronger. They have just given you a grateful gift. Now you can focus your time and best efforts on the people who are more likely to support you.

If there's one behavior that successful leaders own, it's that they know whom to ask, what the right questions are, and when to ask. Do they have some magical power that you don't have because they just always know? Not any more than you. They own their authority by executing one campaign strategy very well: they act from instinct and detach from the outcome. From taking this forward movement, they project their positive result and let it go. They lead with high intention and low attachment—this is their action formula. In other words, their perception of the outcome, regardless of who says what and when in the end, will always be a *yes*, even if it doesn't come directly from the person initially tapped for support or they receive a "Sorry, but now is just not a good time." In their mind, it's still *on the way*. As an everyday habit, they mentally expect their *yes* through some avenue they have yet to discover.

If, in contrast, you were to walk around assuming a negative response at every turn, then you are essentially prequalifying your ask with the belief that it's not something you genuinely believe or deserve. Therefore, you never felt an impulse to act on your instinct, and your overall success rate will drop accordingly.

Why would anyone give you a *yes* if you have rejected yourself in advance? This is a self-sabotaging mindset that everyone experiences, and yet you can pivot away from it and course-correct at any time. Obsessing over your failings is where your ego loves to play and will keep you stuck; your ego can be your own "self-hatred masquerading as self-love."[1]

> When I expect, I always receive. So, I might as well expect a *yes*.

Asking is a nonnegotiable action in your life, and if you're struggling with it, you can begin with introspection—examining your thoughts and emotions. Successful leaders are self-aware. Through self-reflection, they examine who they are, what their values are, and what motivates them. You begin to attract opportunities as soon as you have given yourself the mental nod that you believe in yourself. This fully aligns with the value you have placed on your experience and skill sets. It's not that you are entitled to success; rather, you are substantiating your self-worth in your mind, which drives your success.

The only question you want to ask yourself when kicking off any campaign strategy is, "Do I deserve to lead this new project? Did I earn this promotion?" If the answer is *yes*, lean into it again by asking: "Is this a true statement? Do I believe it?" Until you lock it in as your own truth, don't even attempt to make that outreach phone call or send that email. People will respond to your conviction before you reach out—this is not ego; this is pure instinctive leadership. Others will cheerfully embrace you for who you are when you are glowing under your self-started light.

Asking brings inner peace and joy. Have you ever noticed those who tend to only talk about their next best job, their bigger home, or their upcoming expensive vacations are also consistently unhappy? These folks have never asked themselves the more relevant questions: "What is it that I want? What brings me joy?" Living unconsciously, they tend to run on autopilot to the next big thing they can do or have, never questioning whether they are fully aligned with what makes them happy. Whenever you feel pulled in a new direction for what appears to be no good or rational reason, you are trusting your instincts. You can't explain it. You just know: something good is on the way.

Act in Spite Of

When I returned from maternity leave with my first child, like many first-time parents, I felt a strong sense of regret after three short months—the maximum paid leave given at the time by most companies in the United States. Not willing to accept the status quo for my time off, I called my manager and asked for additional options. I was open to taking unpaid leave or discussing any approach that afforded me more time at home. I soon returned to work with full-time pay, having arranged a remote working agreement that would last for months.

Many of my coworkers scratched their heads over how I pulled that off. At the time, no working parents stayed home one day past their paid maternity leave, and companies offered no flexible alternatives. It was easier to stay silent on the flex-time policy and look the other way. I never questioned it and was empowered to receive more time at home when I had my second child, all because I had raised my hand and asked the first time around. More important, however, this set a precedent for other female leaders in the organization. They too decided to answer the call when growing their families and asked to extend their leave with a full paycheck. Believing their work to stand on its own, they raised their confidence by falling back on years of proving their value and a solid work ethic.

Success lies just outside your comfort zone.

JACK CANFIELD

Today, I can share dozens of stories of professionals who asked and later received. You can apply this principle to your life whenever you find yourself in a challenging situation. Take a step back and ask yourself, "How am I responsible for what I am experiencing, and what do I need to ask to turn it around?" A different response will consistently lead to a wild and different outcome, one that is far better than you expect, when you're willing to stick your neck out just a little and ask for what you want another way.

High Intention, Low Attachment

Asking in business is selling—selling your ideas, selling what you believe—so that eventually you can receive your *yes*. Will everyone always sign up and believe what you believe? Not always. Those who do, you have brought into your vision. When you fearlessly ask for what you want, working this muscle instinctively every day, you inevitably become comfortably confident—asking for more over time, raising the stakes, and negotiating with a high-intention, low-attachment mindset. You get what you need, not what you want. You learn to let go of the outcome because, intuitively, at your core, you know what you need. It may not come immediately, but it will happen when you focus on the higher vision of your life. You reach your goals when you focus on the images you want to create. When negotiating anything in your life, focus on hearing and tasting your *yes*. Asking for resources and later sharing your resources come right around as one sustaining and supportive circle in that way.

THINK LIKE AN IMMIGRANT

My father was an immigrant who picked himself up and out of Sicily to escape poverty. My mother was raised in Brooklyn by her Italian grandparents, who spoke no English. Growing up, I observed my parents giving the shirts off their backs to anyone in need, and yet they weren't too proud to accept acts of charity either and ask for what they needed to support their family.

On our trips to the street markets, I admired how my parents freely exchanged nuggets of information with other immigrants in the neighborhood. They would ask anything and everything, from how to grow the ripest tomatoes to where to find the best shoe store with the finest soles. The street markets were places where everyone depended on one another, not unlike our modern world.

As an observer of these genuine business relationships, I saw how asking never involved a stretch, discomfort, or embarrassment. When you freely desire to help others, you self-qualify to ask—leveraging that classic law of reciprocity that works every time. Performing small acts of service for others brings support to you with equal and positive actions. This makes it so much easier to ask and always expect a positive outcome, not because you deserve it, but because you came from a place without any expectation of gaining.

You become what you believe. If in your ideal vision of the world you see everyone as freely sharing and supporting one another, then you attract the resources and people you need to do just that for you as well, and instinctually, you will know where to find them. As a leader, you empower others to advocate for themselves by serving as that role model. I've coached professionals who often say they struggle with growing their professional network. Yet when I ask how they view this activity, their fixed vision of having empty and dry conversations counters what they would rather experience. It's not until they recognize that when they stick to their true intention—to build authentic relationships that go beyond generic introductions—that they double their network with an approach that now feels natural because they have found other people who share that same desire for a deeper connection.

Immigrants don't have the luxury of thinking through every possible path of opportunity. To survive, they try different avenues until something sticks. They will ask one person to barter and see if they get a response. They will knock on someone's door to see if anyone has a job opportunity. They ask in full expectation of receiving a *yes* and won't hesitate to move on to someone else when they don't, unattached to any stigma of rejection. Immigrants also recognize that success is a numbers game: the more you put yourself out there and ask, the greater is the likelihood that someone will help you, thanks to that law of probability.

Today we tend to stray from relying on others and seeking human interaction. We don't need to ask a grocer which aisle the corn is in anymore; we can order our vegetables online. We don't have to pick up the phone to apply for a job; there's no shortage of self-service tools online that we can use on our own.

While technology has made our lives faster and easier, it has also increased complacency, where we can hold (and hide from) any conversation behind a chat screen, developing a steadily growing e-leadership style we can call our own. Yet technology can never replace the human trust factor that builds relationships. Never underestimate the energy that's formed from in-person interactions that create tight-knit relationships. Fifty years from now, there will still be a need to shake hands, give hugs, or plan an in-person coffee date.

When you think like an immigrant, you worry less about the outcome and what you have to lose and more about the opportunity you can create. Over time, it becomes easy to ask for what you want and care less about the response. The enthusiasm you bring from taking consistent action in this way builds momentum and hence the confidence to stay the course until someone gives you the results you're looking for.

When you find yourself between a rock and a hard place, ask for what you need in spite of any risk of exposure or vulnerability. This is the level of energy you need to bring to the situation to be successful.

In any area of your life where you find yourself resisting something, there is always a payoff. What is the payoff when you wait things out, remain silent, and don't advocate for yourself or your work? The payoff can be folding into a culture that values your being compliant over bringing creative intelligence to your role that may, for example, question the strategic direction taken. While taking this approach may ensure your survival, it also means that you are passing up opportunities to develop any influence or a name for yourself.

Can you think of any success story where choosing to wait on the sidelines for your ideas to be heard turned out to be a winning strategy? Positive outcomes don't happen when you are on a perpetual pause; energy does not shift, and therefore, you cannot create new results.

In Strength Lies Vulnerability

By definition, vulnerability means being capable of or susceptible to being wounded or hurt. No one willingly signs up to be exposed to criticism. You don't wake up in the morning and ask, "With whom should I let my guard down today?" For example, why would you choose to raise your hand when it requires you to reveal a gap in planning? It's a risk to say that you need support in the form of more resources or budget or an external perspective to try to solve a problem. Just getting the words out through admission can be painful. A cry for help can also feel like a stigma that comes with consequences down the road: "He [or she] is a nonstarter."

A challenge many leaders face is not having the best answer in certain situations. Yet, with the dynamics of rapid change in business, it can be impossible to stay relevant and respond with the best solutions without a support system in place. Consider all that you can gain by learning from others and asking for support. Consider the rockstar team you are leading or will lead one day—how will you create a supportive environment for your team to learn and grow if you do not allow yourself to do the same? When you ask something of your team members, the likelihood of their remaining accountable to their decisions is greater when they feel empowered to discover their own solutions, thereby owning their authority.

A good litmus test of your "cry-for-help" barometer is to examine how you would respond if you were on a road trip where you lost your GPS signal. Are you likely to ask someone for directions? If you're the kind of person who prefers to stay the course, potentially risking running out of gas, before pulling over to ask for help, then perhaps that's how you show up asking in your professional life as well.

Often it's more comfortable to ask a stranger than someone you know personally. This could very well be your path of least resistance if you are willing to reach out to someone outside of your inner circle. If you seek out someone to ask for help on the road to get back on course, then you are well positioned to receive a string of positive responses in your life.

There is no shortage of indicators to show how to seek support. Do you tend to read the instruction manual when you don't know how to put something together? Will you invest the time in a self-help book if it is guaranteed to improve your relationships? Notice the patterns of how you have always approached problems. How often had you been willing to change course by asking for help?

Success leaves clues. How frequently you ask for help—and expect to receive it—is a prime predictor of your success. If this is not something you have been comfortable with in the past, there's no time like the present to begin.

If you tend to learn by doing, without instruction or outside help, then this may account for why you generally haven't raised your hand asking for support in the past. Possibly you enjoy experimenting and finding solutions on your own. Though there is nothing wrong with this approach and this is often where your best creativity breaks through, there will come a time when you hit a wall and don't know what to do next. Following a knee-jerk impulse to ask for support, then, may appear in your mind as if you are throwing in the towel. Yet just the opposite is true. It takes guts to step back and seek support—this is what makes us human.

People may admire perfection, but in that same vein, they respect people who are willing to call themselves out and admit to their mistakes or lack of knowledge even more. This is how leaders go from good to great. When you own your authority, you become less concerned with making mistakes because in the back of your mind you can always fall back to a resource that can get you back on track. You see the world as a support system that you can perpetually rely on; successful people surround themselves with people who share this same vision.

Through some strange and powerful principle of
"mental chemistry," which she has never divulged,
Nature wraps us in the impulse of strong desire
which recognizes no such word as impossible
and accepts no such reality as failure.

NAPOLEON HILL

Is it normal to walk around expecting everything to work out? As a leader committed to remaining intentional, why not? We have been conditioned from childhood to ask for things that never panned out, that we should assume failure, so we can say, "I knew it wouldn't work out." This is no more than your ego trying to protect you. Being rejected, however, can be leveraged as the fuel to keep you going and build momentum. In reality, there is no such thing as failure. You merely keep trying different things and see which approach sticks so that you can reroute.

A law of physics states that energy must be in motion to create a new result or reaction. Similarly, the act of trying and seeing where an idea lands is how you remain in motion to achieve the things you want. These are the experiences from which you learn. When things don't work out as you expect, you can lean into your instincts, which guide you to change course or try something else. This is why external feedback is so crucial to this process. Ironically, we seldom hesitate to ask on behalf of others who need our support; yet we don't have the same inclination when it comes to advocating for ourselves. To test this theory, consider this question: How likely would you respond to a friend who, as a favor, asks you to float his or her name around to find a new position. Turning that request around, how likely is it that you would do the same outreach on behalf of yourself?

Your beliefs, behaviors, and images of your future are the only things you have any control over. Change your thoughts on what you expect when you ask, and change your results and your life.

NO IS NEXT

There are three types of people you can ask for support: those who agree to help in some way, those who turn you down with a straight *no* or *not now*, and those who have already given you the *yes* in their mind but are wired to push back anyway and say *no* regardless of anything you say or do. They only want to see how you handle it and to awaken a persistence in you or possibly just to help you stretch. These folks could be coming from a good place; perhaps that's how they earned their own stripes, or they have an innate need to protect themselves by resisting being the resident pushover, being perceived as the weak *yes*-person. Others may give you a veiled *no* until you can prove that your proposal is watertight or crystallize how you'll make it a win-win for their own initiatives.

In any difficult situation where you don't receive what you expect, take a step back and recognize that this is part of the process—embrace it for what it is. When something doesn't pan out, we often react automatically and assume failure when, in reality, it's a lesson learned. Any perceived roadblock is merely a signal telling you to reroute and try something else. This is when you are being called on to try something new and different, which is often a better opportunity. It just hasn't presented itself to you in that way—yet. When we are not tuned into and trusting our instincts, we are only focused on what *is* as opposed to what's *possible* to create. Anything that you are trying to strong-arm only pushes it further away by raising resistance to the object of desire. Letting go to reassess and try another approach or staying the course with a fresh approach to how you're trying to sell it may be all you need. What's the next step that you can take that would feel light and free flowing with ease? What does your gut say when you ask the question?

The reality is that people who say *no* and mean *no* are only building your momentum to keep on asking until you receive the *yes* you need. Either way, trust your instincts, and keep moving ahead, creating your own path, or reroute somewhere along the way. Embrace these people and thank them. Either you will prove your value and earn their trust over time, or you will move on to those who will partner with you instead.

Not receiving the results we expect can feel like defeat and negatively influence so much of our behavior because of a fear of rejection and a sense of losing our self-worth when we hear it. Yet, in reality, these rejecters have just saved us so much time that you otherwise would have lost. This doesn't mean that your result can't happen or that you're not good enough. It means that you have to wait a little longer before you try again. It means that you have to go in at another time and ask the question in a different way. It means that you need to move to a place where you can calmly ask, "What can I learn from this experience?" and "Is this feedback I need to hear?" Work it like a muscle that will make you stronger, and you will become very creative at how to realize self-created opportunities instead that will help you grow.

Answer the Objections

What would be some logical reasons for others not to buy into what you are proposing? As a leader, it's your job to take responsibility for your results by knowing your clients well enough to understand what their concerns are and to prepare and address them. In other words you have to answer your clients' objections.

You own your authority when you prepare for this kind of conversation if those justifications arise because you will have rehearsed and responded to those areas of concern well ahead of time. To walk away owning that conversation, you have to know yourself and know where your clients stand at the same time, tailoring what you say to the results they want to hear you focus on.

The reality is that when you either ask for or negotiate anything in your career, your job is to help your clients see how you can be part of their bigger vision and success. When you approach others in this way, you quickly develop creative ways to guarantee their buy-in to working with you.

If you do not come to a compromise or some agreement, you can find someone else with whom you can partner. You can put yourself in your client's shoes and consider what you can do differently to encourage him or her to work with you. You can turn any situation around and take *no* to seek the next opportunity. Let's look at some success stories from the application of the *no*-is-next formula:

- Stephen King's bestselling first book, *Carrie,* was rejected 30 times, with one publisher saying it was "not interested in science fiction which deals with negative utopias. They do not sell."[2] Losing faith, King tossed his manuscript in the trash (which was later rescued by his wife). He finally put aside his self-doubt and continued to resubmit to publishers.
- Michael Jordan was cut from his high school basketball team. "I have missed over 9,000 shots in my career and lost almost 300 games. . . . I have failed over and over and over again in my life. And that is why I succeed."[3]
- A little-known fact about star baseball player Babe Ruth is that he once held the record for strikeouts with 1,330 of them. "Every strike brings me closer to the next home run."[4]
- Steven Spielberg had wanted to go to "the prestigious film schools at the University of Southern California and the University of California, Los Angeles, but, ironic as it may seem in retrospect, he was rejected at both film schools."[5]

PERFECTLY POLITE PUSHBACK

Until you choose to speak up and ask for what you want—whether it will be in the form of support, a commitment, or an approval of a new initiative—you are passing up ripe opportunities to gain influence in your career. It's a fine balance as a leader to be authentic, human, and agreeable while under pressure to perform. Following your instinct can take the form of remaining easy and approachable to seek more influence; yet this may not yield the results you're looking for when you are campaigning for your team or the direction you believe is in the best interest of the organization.

When you don't ask, you don't receive. The hidden cost of not stepping up to advocate for yourself, of not asking for the *yes* of others, is that others will assume and fully expect the *yes* from you, thereby not protecting your time and priorities, including those of your team. Lacking pushback chops can put you at risk of being perceived as a *yes*-person.

Once you become comfortable asking for and fully expecting to receive a *yes*, you become so accustomed and desensitized to the process that you learn to reverse it as well. You become very good at setting boundaries with others around your time and work. If you consider yourself to be someone who too often agrees with everyone or there is a people-pleasing factor at play, then I invite you to experiment with saying *no* and pushing back on people. Here, too, you can develop an instinctive muscle to protect both you and your team. This is strong mental and physical energy that honors the structure in your life by protecting your personal power. Many people walk around not knowing what they want, which makes it easy for them to fold into and satisfy other people's agendas instead of becoming clear and following through on their own intentions and desires.

If you fail to plan, you are planning to fail!
BENJAMIN FRANKLIN

Stagnation from being motionless and not reaching out for support can keep you stuck emotionally and create a self-fulfilling prophecy that replays the same results with no expectation of progress. It isn't too difficult to find people who complain about the things that they don't have or that have gone wrong. Leaders who become comfortable asking for support are also communicating their trust in someone by nature of the very question. This then raises a question for you as well: How well do you trust in your ability to lead? How well you trust yourself is directly related to how willing you are to take risks. The more risks you take, the more confidence you build. The more confidence you build, the stronger you stand behind your decisions and vision.

You learn to respectfully "agree to disagree" so well that you shield yourself from getting swept away by other people's energy, succumbing to their power. You can freely point others to someone else when you need to, preserving your focus and ability to do more of your own great work. As a result, that *yes*, which you fully expect to receive, creates a magnificent check and balance system in this way.

Asking for what you want is not a magic bullet. It's a muscle—the more you use it consistently, the stronger you become. If you haven't ridden a bike in more than 20 years, do you need to be trained again? Your body knows the truth; it will know what to do and move instinctively when it needs to. The same applies when you ask for help as a leader; you allow yourself to be bold and to some extent vulnerable, trusting yourself enough to ask the question.

If you have some fear around asking for what you want, ask for the smaller things you know that people can give you. Practice this new-found behavior on those you consider to be your low-hanging fruit. The more you receive what you want in a place that feels safe, the more you can confidently ramp up and instinctually ask for bigger things that require a deeper plunge of discomfort.

Great athletes implement this technique consistently when they are training to win. Once they achieve a steady string of triumphs, they strengthen their self-discipline and train even harder, holding themselves more accountable. They understand that they must be mentally strong to handle risks and setbacks such as injuries, failures, close calls, and fluctuating emotions from a crowd.

History has proved that the more victories you have beneath your belt, the more likely and confident you will feel to take a chance, banking on you to achieve even more. The law of probability teaches that when you cast your net often to catch potential opportunities, you are more likely to achieve positive results—not just any results, however, but results that you have designed intentionally.

BUY-IN WITH PLEASANT PERSISTENCE

It can be mentally draining to repeatedly rely on other business areas to get your projects done. This can be requesting the hire of an additional resource or jump-starting a new project, for example. You've done your due diligence and held a few meetings, and your team has sent a flotilla of reminder emails still showing that no progress has been made. Now what?

There's a soft and direct way to get the other team to help in checking the boxes your client needs you to check. Calmly state the circumstances: (1) give a current snapshot of where you are, (2) move on to the opportunities for the team leader to take action on what you require, and (3) close with the risks of this action being delayed (e.g., the risk of losing more time). This last step is essential to emphasize because it turns your problem around and over to his or her side of the table, no longer making the situation solely your problem. A pull strategy you can use to have the team consider ways in which they can now help you is to lead with the words, "What would have to happen . . . ?"

"What would have to happen to get an additional resource?"

"What would have to happen to make this project milestone by next week?"

"How do you feel about us escalating to your boss to help us accomplish this?"

You can use this buy-in technique when you hit a dead end with someone who could otherwise release the resources you need. This can also be where all the chips are down and you openly state that you are going around that person to get the work completed, allowing him or her the opportunity to take action one last time. Essentially, you pivot the problem and pull that person over to your side of the table, asking, "What would have to happen if . . . ?" and "How do you feel about . . . ?" The other person is now in a position to move to where you find yourself and try to solve the problem with you. In other words, it is no longer a weight sitting on your shoulders.

If he or she is resistant to pushing along your agenda, this buy-in strategy still works. It works because of the intention behind "suggestology." Energetically, the person feels that you are no longer accepting *no* or any further postponement. You are action oriented and now nominating the person to support you without covertly going around him or her. Consider this a gentle elbow nudge that encourages a sense of urgency for that person to act now.

This approach has him or her helping you find a solution to the problem, and no longer are you on your own and without the person's assistance. You are not resorting to aggressively or abrasively pushing your way through but instead soliciting his or her support by raising your concern that it now becomes the person's responsibility as well. Asking for buy-in in this way is one method where you can be fully transparent with no hidden agenda and own your power.

If you find yourself coming up against leadership that chooses to ignore the red flags you are raising, it may be time to shake things up to support the greater whole—your project, your team, and the organization as a whole. If, for example, your team is experiencing heavy stress from rapid-fire drills with little or no attention to increasing budget or resources, pivot and bring those decision makers over to your side with the "help-me-to-help-you" strategy.

Put yourself in the organization's shoes, answering that key question: "So what?" Why should it care if the members of your team may have reached a breaking point that affects their health? Why should the organization care if everyone is putting in 60-hour workweeks to make their deliverables? From its corner of the world, the business will carry on as usual as long as the precedent has been set that you and/or your team will "figure it out" at any cost.

Turn this around: How can you make the people in the organization care? Go back in there with a few clear-cut reasons why they should care. Answering the "So what?" question is taking responsibility as a leader. It takes one person to shift a workplace culture by putting his or her neck on the line.

Putting yourself in your manager's shoes is being sensitive to and aware of what his or her risks are if you were in their position to make a decision and instinctively act. There may very well be some level of fear and uncertainty in making the tough decisions you're asking for. Paint the picture of exactly what will be affected for your manager (not you) and stamp a guarantee of failed results because the work is not feasible given the timing, vacation, effort, etc. Inform him or her of what projects will be delayed and what you are proposing, not as a long-term commitment but as a short-term stopgap.

What is the path of least resistance people in the organization can take right now? Give them some options with which they can work, the short-term/less-than-three-months commitment, so that it doesn't seem so scary of a commitment for them to press "Go." Also give them the long-term roadmap that they can revisit in one year, which your red flag recommendations can successfully set them up for if they heed your advice.

Before your meeting closes, frame up the major points so that your listeners are clear on the promised results and opportunities, and then point out the risks and reel them back in, making it a win-win for all. Whether your audience is open-eared and listening or resistant to change, you have an opportunity to own your authority and influence.

If, as a leader, you're willing to take this kind of instinctive action and you still don't receive any response to the icebergs you have raised, then you may have an underlying issue here. Is this a culture where you will grow your career and advance? What is your gut telling you about where you will thrive in your career and whether your ideas will be heard? Will this culture support the balance you seek among work, family, and a healthy lifestyle?

However, if you find yourself in quicksand, being set up for failure consistently, then it's likely time to weigh your options. What's the risk if you stay in a role where you are feeling stale and stagnant? Are you ready to find an environment where you will have an impact and grow in leadership?

SHAKESPEAREAN CONFIDENCE

*Our doubts are traitors and cause us to miss the good
we oft might win, by fearing to attempt.*
WILLIAM SHAKESPEARE

As our beloved Shakespeare once taught—to get the part, you must first own the part. If you are experiencing any anxiety from asking for support, then you can learn to reverse any negative outcome by envisioning that discussion free flowing with ease. Visualization is a fast-path tool that leverages your mind to translate any thought to reality, and it has been shown to reduce anxiety while doing so. When you visualize yourself sitting at the table with confidence, fully expecting to receive the outcome you want, you can feel that it's on the way, strengthening your body to prepare for that conversation.

There are many ways to lock in the images that you want to create in your life. Journaling your thoughts can evoke feelings of success because of the power of focus and the creative stimulation it stirs toward finding a solution. You can give your brain the images it needs to focus by developing a *mind movie* that you can replay consistently until the line between imagination and reality is too blurred to distinguish one from the other.

Increasing your body's energy is another powerful strategy you can use before you "switch on" to negotiate anything that holds meaning for you. You can hop on a treadmill or do some morning stretches to circulate body energy before making that key phone call. Showing up with high energy will allow you to stay the course and speak calmly—keep it slow and steady.

How passionate you are and how included you make people feel in the room dictate how successful you will be speaking in that room. We often worry more about the words we choose and how we sound versus what's relevant to the listener. This not only lowers our energy, weakening our bodies, but also dilutes our value. Being clear on your intention creates the passion others feel around your very ask. It's also what keeps you in their minds for new opportunities for years to come. By asking for what you need and projecting an impressive belief in your vision, you can become great at advocating for yourself and others. You don't have to sell it; you own the room by leading with your intention and in spite of any pushback.

To walk away with a successful compromise with anyone, consider a *yes* that would work for both of you. Start with the bare minimum that you want to achieve, and then inch it up a notch, imagining an ideal outcome where you both stand to gain. You're not there to force anyone's hand. Keep your intention at the forefront as you engage, but know that a successful outcome can look like many things. It can be receiving less now with the insight and intuition for building more buy-in later on.

Consider the what-if fear that could instinctively nudge you into taking action. It's not meant to be a roadblock but can be used as a signal to help you make a decision. Keep the following question present when you face a difficult decision or need to ask for backup to support a goal: "Who else is going to ask on your behalf except you?"

Calibrating Emotional Energy

Is your performance typically higher during in-person meetings versus those held over the phone? Do you feel more confident after going for a swim or finishing a heart-pumping morning run? Notice how you feel as you go about your daily routine.

We tend to pay more attention to achieving our desired outcomes than imagining what they would feel like when we experience them. Focusing on the images that you need in order to create your outcomes is effective because it helps you put yourself emotionally into the future you want to create. In other words, you can *feel* your way there. The best way to do this is to tap into your emotions and the energy they release. Emotional people get things faster—this is true for both positive and negative thinking. This is the reason why those who are stressed out all the time are constantly getting physically sick and feeling mentally drained. This is also why expressing out loud positive affirmations before you walk into a situation you would otherwise wish to avoid can swiftly turn that event into a supportive space. There is no greater way to shape your mind's internal monologue than speaking and hearing your own words.

Having emotional self-control is the ability to manage how you react to what is happening in your environment at any moment in time. It's what determines whether you have a response or a reaction to an event and is a contributing factor to self-leadership. Leading effectively is handling difficult circumstances, reducing conflict, and addressing differences through conversation, all of which require emotion management.

> *Act as if what you do makes a difference. It does.*
> WILLIAM JAMES

Most people ask and then disengage, walking away assuming that the results they want can't happen. When managing your emotions, you can act as if what you want has already been delivered. Owning your authority as a leader is going against the grain when you are precisely at that breaking point and want to throw up your hands and give up. Yet it's during these pivotal moments that you are being challenged to keep going and follow through on your instincts.

So how do you get there, especially if your present reality looks so different from what you want? Start with spending a few minutes each day considering what the intention behind your visualization of the ideal outcome is, and then take inventory of your emotions as a check: How do you feel?

There is a set of distinct emotions that you can tap into that influence your sense of owning your power in any setting. It's called the *emotional guidance scale.*[6] This is a grid that ranks human emotions with varying levels of energy frequency. The emotional state you are in ensures that any intention you have will be realized as long as you are in a state of consciousness. You are living consciously when you are fully awake and aware of your thoughts, emotions, and surroundings, including those you are engaging with. Your body and everything around you are composed of atoms vibrating at different frequencies. When you are experiencing the emotion of joy, you are vibrating at a higher frequency level than, for example, a state of feeling jealousy. Joy and happiness can have you feel more connected to everything around you and change your perception of how to handle a given circumstance. Choosing positive thoughts and feelings essentially aligns with the cells in your body, influencing them to function in their most optimal state and contributing to a sense of feeling good versus bad. It's what ultimately drives your perspective of future events, and whether you would expect your actions and future outlook to have either a positive or negative outcome.

Thoughts of envy, hopelessness, and anger also have a direct impact on your body. These low-lying negative emotions raise the potential for your body to experience illness and disease due to their lower vibrational frequency. This is why those who give their ear and attention to negative past events that may have hurt them are consistently feeling stressed out and as a result consistently getting sick and face a new set of negative circumstances that fire off, much like a chain reaction.

Identifying your emotions with a positive or negative energy flow can help you shift from suffering red-hot anger or loss and disappointment to feeling an elevated sense of purpose and enthusiasm.

Whenever you are experiencing a negative feeling, pause and ask yourself where that emotion lies on the emotional guidance scale. Thoughts evoking contentment, optimism, passion, freedom, love, appreciation, and gratefulness would rank significantly higher than thoughts of insecurity, guilt, unworthiness, worry, and anxiety. That's not to say you won't ever experience these feelings; you are human. Should you experience a low-lying negative emotion however, try to find thoughts that feel slightly better from that set point until you can climb your way up to a higher emotional frequency that feels slightly better, opening up a next best course of action that can lead to a feeling of enthusiasm and encouragement, thereby owning your power. If you are anywhere on an emotional level such as boredom or lower, then right before a key meeting or conversation, reschedule it. You will not achieve the results you were looking for. It will end in frustration from falling short of expectation, pushing you further lower on the emotional spectrum. Energetically, it's impossible to achieve any success in this situation because vibrationally you are pushing away the things that you want and are not aligned with a desired outcome that would otherwise have the potential to be achieved if you felt lined up with it. It's a disconnect that will only widen until you are able to recalibrate your emotions, which can take some time. You may need to leave a room, go for a walk or a drive—disconnect to reconnect later when you feel more grounded and balanced to have a conversation.

Consider whenever you are feeling cold in a room. You might raise the thermostat to a higher temperature to feel more comfortable. The same applies with your emotions. You see this regularly when you attempt to a read a room for the first time. You walk into a new setting such as a meeting, an interview, a celebration, or someone's home for the first time. You read the room to determine the mood of those gathered there. Is it the right time to have a conversation? Does everyone seem on edge? Do people appear to enjoy themselves, and if so, will you fit in? Effective leaders go above and beyond just reading the temperature of their environment; they set the thermostat on how they want themselves, their teams, and their clients to feel. They determine and set the bar for the atmosphere they want others to experience around them. This isn't possible unless you can recalibrate emotionally in an environment.

Your intention to create positive, forward-looking outcomes is only possible when you are able to enter a situation with encouraging expectation. Whatever you want and are asking for will fall flat and on deaf ears with those you engage unless you can shift to a state of hopefulness or above and change course before asking for the *yes*. This is why it is so important to you as a leader to be aware of how you feel. Think of your energy level, emotions, and actions as all being lined up to support your North Star and indicate how you can stay agile as a leader. Being centered, sensing the energy in the room, and then transforming that feeling into action have the power to inspire those who follow your lead.

Also, give careful consideration to the time of day when you seek some form of support. Are you a morning or an afternoon person? Follow your instinct on this one—what's the best time for you to feel the most grounded and centered? Choose when you believe your ask will support you and remain intentional around that window of opportunity. We easily get caught up in how we sound and what we have to contribute but rarely put emphasis on our environment and how naturally our bodies perform better during certain times of the day.

When you are asked what time works best to schedule a meeting, take a few minutes before you respond, and quietly lean into your body. What time do you instinctively feel would work well for you? When are you typically more focused? When would your audience be the most receptive to you? Doing a little homework, you can learn someone's preferred time of day and when he or she is at the peak of performance. When would be the best time to get someone's ear so that the person would likely give you a *yes*?

A study was done inside a courtroom relating to this timing strategy in which the number of paroles granted by a judge was summarized throughout the day. The results showed a high-flying continuous *yes* pattern right after a judge's morning and afternoon meals. Yet, as the day proceeded, paroles granted were shown to take a deep dive and consistently flatline until the end of the day.[7] While you can't predict the outcomes, it pays to consider moving the time for when you instinctively feel your performance would best be received.

THE MEETING BEFORE THE MEETING

An often-overlooked yet powerful opportunity for reaping an abundant crop of *yes*es occurs when you arrive for a conversation a few minutes ahead of the actual meeting start time and engage in small talk. There is no better place to engage someone before you talk shop than a meeting before the meeting.

The meeting before the meeting is an opportune and instinctive strategy that works this way: Say, for example, you are scheduled to attend a meeting at 11 a.m. and instead show up at 10:55 a.m. with your coffee in one hand and your notepad in the other hand. Setting them carefully down on the table, you talk about your weekend, you talk about your kids, or you talk about anything that makes you glow with pride. If the manager or client with whom you are meeting also has kids, plays tennis, or enjoys cooking as much as you do, find that common ground and open up the gates to a free-flowing conversation, chatting casually around your shared interests. This sets up an environment that is upbeat and makes everyone comfortable. When you come from a place of being open-eared and curious to learn more about someone, that again is energy people will feel immediately.

Engaging teachers and trainers also implement this strategy as participants float into their classrooms and workshops. Once the participants take a seat, the teacher or trainer swings by, introduces himself or herself, and asks the participants to share a little about themselves and why they have signed up. This not only puts the teacher or trainer at ease but also allows him or her to instinctively navigate the content of these quick and valuable meet-and-greets. In the professional speaking world, this is known as *warming up* an audience to better gain a pulse on the energy of the room. The same applies to your key conversations. What would have to happen for you to feel like you are successfully warming up the room with your clients? Before I jump into any coaching session, whether it's a one-on-one or I'm leading a group, the first questions I ask are "What's new and good? What are you grateful for?" This is a ritual that clears the space before the participants dive into specific career challenges. It also allows them to honor and celebrate wherever they are on their career path, acknowledging that a slow and steady pace wins the race. The same applies to where you are right now. What are you celebrating in any area of your life?

When I took my son to his first soccer practice, I arrived 15 minutes early to let him kick the ball around with the other players, get to know his team, and ease any fears he may have had. This also allowed me the opportunity to speak to the coach, introduce myself, learn his style, share a little background on my son's athletic history, and ask any questions before practice started. Creating the meeting before the meeting applies everywhere, beyond strictly your career.

> When you show up for the meeting before the meeting, you warm up and establish a calm and steady dialogue in which you can stand your ground confidently and with full intention.

Pitch it until you stick it. Not every idea that you have is going to stick whenever you throw it out. Whether your ideas are embraced at every turn is unimportant. What matters is that you find your voice each time. In other words, you are comfortable thinking out loud, sharing those ideas, and putting your thoughts out there until one of them sticks. When you don't get the positive feedback that you were hoping for, try pitching an idea a different way. Everything is feedback, and you can change your pitch or question to get the response that you want next time, perhaps from learning more about your client's needs and where you can add value.

Consistently asking is a leadership tool that will support you throughout your career and life. It's how you build confidence that leads to making better decisions because you're taking on smart risk. You create small wins over time and grow further, increasing your confidence and risk tolerance. You have more courage and become more comfortable in your decisions over time.

Yet it's not so much on the outcome that successful leaders stay focused on. It's also the culture they want to build to remain relevant in an organization. You increase your influence when you invite peers to take on risk with you, engaging them to understand and be similarly comfortable making decisions where advocating for themselves and accepting risk are assumed. Those most willing to follow your lead can model this for others on the team, helping them step into trusting their instincts as well.

Everyone, including you, has a personal law of averages to work with. Recall the success formula for sales leaders—they will sign on one new client for every sixth phone call they make. This means that if you want a steady pipeline of new and impactful opportunities to lead, it is nonnegotiable that you must inch up your asking.

When we reflect on how we were perceived as children, we often recall how we were up for anything and could pick up new habits easily without concern for how things turned out. When we got older, however, we lost our flexibility and became resistant to change. When you ask for what you want, approach others with the curiosity of your seven-year-old self, unattached to the outcome, and with the same intensity of desire and persistence that you had when you were young.

You get what you think about. When you open the windows and ask for support, you may receive a thought impulse to pick up the phone to call a dormant client, ask for someone's point of view on a dilemma, or hire a coach. This is your instinct speaking to you, not because those calls to action were always whispering in your ear but because you found the courage to ask the question first and have a curious mind with an approach of "Let's see what I can create from taking this action."

The Power of Writing Down Your Goals

There is no playbook on how to ask. You can ask by looking in the mirror each morning. And you can ask by journaling precisely what you wish to accomplish that day. Writing down your thoughts will exponentially help you accelerate the things you want because it enables you to focus on those ideal images and feelings engaging the 17-second energy principle.[8] If you hold a thought for 17 seconds or more, you set in motion the energy to create that desire, which makes it stronger. Should your emotion lie within a low-frequency range where you are feeling drained or frozen, you can use the 17-second window to "lift your spirits" by thinking a more positive thought and raise your emotion. This consistent recalibration may seem awkward at first, but it can help you tap into your instincts to align with the inspired actions you feel from processing your thoughts in this way. It's why writing is so effective in gaining clarity on your goals, which makes them that much more real. Writing engages sharp focus because it easily helps you pass that 17-second mark and create images that line up with your train of thought—images that no longer seem an impossible stretch to create. You have locked those visuals in your mind where they now become your truth.

In a scientific study conducted at Dominican University of California, psychology professor Gail Matthews found that you become 42 percent more likely to achieve your goals simply by writing them down on a regular basis.[9] Consider attaching an image next to your goals and view them all at least three times a day. Sit back and watch how greater your success will be when you make this a consistent daily practice. You can begin each day by making instinctual requests based on your need for support and then act on those inspired impulses right away. Consider the areas of your life where you stopped yourself from asking and outcomes took a U-turn away from what you wanted. On reflection, were you following your instincts at the time?

What is it costing you not to advocate for yourself? What would be the benefit if you did?

Find Your Zen: Your Environment Supports Positive Action

Your environment is a contributing factor to why you may not be advocating enough for yourself. If I did a surprise inspection of your home, what would it look like? Are there place settings on your kitchen table? Is your bookshelf tidy and organized? Would you lead me to a room that you call your own that inspires the next chapter of your life? If not, would I see a cluttered dining table serving as a makeshift desk and office? Would I meet a grumpy naysayer who lives with you and brings you down at every turn?

Your personal space can play a significant role in holding you back in life and can further feed into habits that keep you stuck, inevitably showing up when you are leading in any area of your life, family, or career alike. We tend to accept our surroundings and experience for what they are rather than addressing them and recognizing how they can keep us from creating the outcomes we want. A cluttered environment also prohibits you from asking.

We would rather live in our comfort zone and keep things the same than act on our gut desire to create change, even though our instincts are a trusted source that nudges us to do the very things that will support us. Often when we fall into complacency, we tend to seek ways to become motivated again in order to mobilize and get back on track. However, if you take just one simple action, such as going for a walk or listening to music, you'll find that this becomes your motivation (and momentum) to do more. In other words, seeking motivation externally from someone or something does not inspire you to move. It's the *movement*, the energy shift that creates the *motive* to keep going, harnessing new energy and therefore more movement. You likely have experienced this "passive-versus-active" energy at play when you set a daily exercise goal, running 20 minutes on the treadmill, for example. Then one day, you don't feel very motivated to stick to that practice and you stop training. If, however, you found the slightest inclination to simply step onto the belt and press "Start," those next 20 minutes would flow effortlessly, but it wouldn't happen until you took action first.[10] Likewise, stepping outside of the house, with an intention just to get some fresh air for a few minutes to clear your head, can turn into a power hour of mental wellness where you will reset and feel revitalized.

When you tolerate an environment that doesn't ground you and nurture your potential, subconsciously, it will also stop you from acting on the things that you want to achieve. Likewise, when you are focused on things that you no longer want to experience, including a toxic work environment, similar circumstances inevitably surround you until you choose to step away.

To create a supportive personal space for yourself, you can start with recognizing the things for which you have made allowances and that now need to go. These are the things in your life that are distracting you from what you want to create for yourself. It could be a disorganized garage, a challenging relationship, or an overhaul of your filing system. These all contribute to an unstructured environment that will pull your attention away from what you should be focusing on—your goals, real desires you can achieve that will stretch and not freeze you.

When you walk into your office, do you feel excited to be there? Environments have a psychological impact. It could be low ceilings, office design, lighting, or the number of windows allowing sunlight in—all these things can affect your attitude, directly influencing your performance levels and the productivity of your team.

When we accept a negative environment in our daily lives, we fall back to a resignation state in which we don't get the collaboration we hope for and continue to tolerate relationships that no longer support us. Our mindset at the time is, "Well, if employee turnover keeps growing, then how am I supposed to accomplish bigger projects ahead? How does that impact my health and my personal goal to spend more time with family?" Feeding these thoughts can have you quickly turn to self-defeat mode. Be aware of your environment and how it makes you feel; this includes how you keep your car, your desk—even a fresh, clean refrigerator counts. In recent years, we have seen an influx of home organization toolkits to help us feel restored and hopeful. Applying consistent, clutter-free techniques to your personal space can keep your mind stress free. When you tolerate cluttered living spaces or unfinished projects, you tend to feel more fatigued and resigned to current circumstances rather than leading with a plan and taking action. This impacts your productivity, focus, attitude, and propensity to advocate for yourself.

Consider small ways to create swift changes in the energy of your environment. This can be giving appreciation to an employee for his or her performance, buying a coffee for a stranger, or donating your time as a mentor to younger professionals. Instinctively embracing a random positive act of service is a choice you can make every day. In any moment, when you act with an intention to feel good and be in a state of high and purposeful expectation, you'll find that more people will want to work with you.

Nurturing a positive environment and mindset is the basis of the practice of *feng shui*, which promises that you will attract beneficial energy known as strong *chi* into your home or office via the positioning of objects to harness that energy. *Chi* is positive energy and is continuously moving and changing. It's a force field that you feel around you that makes you feel either good or bad in a particular space.

It helps you to:

- Clear the clutter in your home or office.
- Get good-quality air and light in your space.
- Be mindful of the quality of energy in your life.
- Allow good airflow through your doors and windows.

The energy that you create in your home or office matters because it will accumulate in the objects around you, further raising your confidence levels. When you have a robust and vibrant flow of *chi* in your environment, you tap into the power of focus and feel supported in achieving the goals you have envisioned for yourself.

There's no secret sauce: you own your authority by caring about how you feel. This includes nurturing your environment and relationships, the first being the one you have with yourself. This is how you find and acquire the things you want in your life. This is how you take responsibility for the results you want to achieve. This is how you move into a state of flow, increasing your influence with opportunities that keep you growing.

> *Go! Go! Go! It makes no difference where just so you go!*
> *Remember, at the first opportunity, go.*
>
> JEANETTE RANKIN

SPEAKING
WITHOUT APOLOGY

On November 21, 1934, Ella Fitzgerald made her singing debut at age 17 during one of the amateur nights held at the Apollo Theater. She was a dancer and had planned to strut her moves on stage. She was so nervous that at the last minute she followed her gut and decided to sing instead, won the talent contest, and went on to become one of the world's greatest jazz singers.

QUIET POWER

Every time you open your mouth . . . you display . . .
your exact stock of knowledge or your lack of it!
Genuine wisdom is usually conspicuous
through modesty and silence.
NAPOLEON HILL

Whenever I tell people how important it is to be more visible in their career, while in agreement, they will admit that they don't necessarily walk out the door each morning setting out to be on anyone's radar. In an ideal world, most people would be satisfied to hunker down to do their jobs well in quiet bliss as long as their work is appreciated and they can add value for others. I knew this all too well. I was one of these low-key souls until I learned how to speak without apology. I recognized early in my career, when I was just out of college, that I would either sink or swim as soon as I began working in the "wild west" of equities trading. Because I was so green, the concept of thinking on my feet seemed like a high-stakes gamble, with an undeniable feeling of being underqualified that swept over me at every turn. When you're under pressure to perform, you learn to move fast and find your voice if you are willing to hold the line and step into your fears. For many people, the psychology behind having a deadline can also be motivating and just the nudge they need to keep their feet to the fire.

There's an unspoken freeze factor that takes place after you make any major career milestone that should come with a "proud me" pause for celebration. You can follow the playbook, land the right position, make the connections you need, roll up your sleeves, work hard, and make all the right career moves, including achieving a promotion or that next leadership opportunity, only to suddenly shift into reverse, with self-doubt creeping in: "So, I got here, but do I really deserve it?"

Imagine that just yesterday the answer was a *yes*. Yet here you are today, walking around not fully owning your authority. Keeping to a certain script is one reason why we hold ourselves back from finding our voice. We believe that if we walk into a room and whip out the right cue card, prepared for every question, then we are home free. Yet when we're on the hook to sell that next major presentation, we can spiral into panic mode and freeze. There's a belief that whatever we did to get to our next position was somehow the result of beating the system with the odds in our favor and suppressing our inner belief in ourselves.

There's an unspoken leadership component to owning your personal power; it's called *speaking without apology*. It's confidently communicating with an unwavering faith and quiet resilience in what you have to say and why your words matter. It's also looking back at the success you've had in your career and recognizing what has always worked for you so that you can repeat your results. By focusing on what has worked for you, you claim your personal success factors. If your tendency is to think first and speak later, then own that. Taking a two-second pause before you speak commands quiet power every time. You say more by saying less. If writing is your primary form of communication through quiet reflection, let it flow. Those written words will help formulate what you want to say verbally. If you find that your energy source flows best from digging into information before engaging in conversation, there too don't question it; leverage what's worked well and own it.

> *I cannot give you the formula for success,*
> *but I can give you the formula for failure, which is:*
> *Try to please everybody.*
> HERBERT SWOPE

There is language that we consistently use that is diluting our message and weakening our position. It takes the form of speech qualifiers that unknowingly roll off our tongues yet take away our best power and energy. This language feeds into a sorry syndrome where we at times feel compelled to apologize when we speak up. Men and women at any level of leadership are shown to struggle with it. The most frequent and observable way you can hear it at play on any given day is in the use of the word *just*.

"I'm just checking in" or "I'm just calling because . . ." seems to signal an apologetic stance where you don't wish to inconvenience someone or possibly feel a need to explain yourself while in fact you are weakening yourself. Turning that language around, you can say instead, "Catch me up on how our project stands" or "I'm calling to let you know that I will be late for the meeting." In this way, you bring an entirely different energy to the conversation because you are not questioning yourself or anyone else. You are stating your intention and standing confidently behind your words irrespective of how they sound or may be received. Calling in to let someone know that you will be late is how you remain responsible and stand in integrity. You are neither minimizing yourself for being delayed nor blaming yourself for calling as the sender of bad news. Speaking without apology is affirming what you need to say, staying true to your words, and letting go.

There's also language we use that undermines our value when we give too much explanation. For example, if you were running late to a morning meeting and you show up at the office and say to your peers, "I'm sorry I'm late, but I had a doctor's appointment." How does that feel compared with saying instead, "Good morning, I had a dentist appointment earlier. Catch me up."

In the former statement, through use of the word *but*, you're responding to a concern that was never expressed; yet you feel compelled to answer: "Where were you?" In the latter, you are acknowledging where you were and why you were late, moving on to business. You kept it light and airy. The more you talk about something, the more attention you give it. You have stated the circumstance and taken responsibility as opposed to shrugging it off.

We also see weak language show up when we're indecisive about a course of action, unable to pick a lane to direct our team's efforts. We may also wait too long and become reluctant to answer a question or second-guess ourselves, both of which weaken your authority. When you don't have enough information to rely on, you want to trust your instincts and communicate that decision with confidence.

Speaking without apology creates a mindset shift in how you see yourself and whether your self-image is one of weakness or strength. When you speak without apology, notice how your body feels. Although these corrections are subtle tweaks of language, they can completely transform the dynamics of a conversation and how you feel physically.

Leading well is essential, but it's not enough to be successful. Whenever you're taking on more leadership, you want to be perceived to do it well. Be comfortable owning your expertise. If you were to measure your success using this approach, your only yardstick is being honest with yourself—how often do you speak up so that there's no doubt in anyone's mind about what you bring to the table? Although speaking up is essential, it stretches beyond contributing to conversations and chiming in with recommendations. I'm speaking of the kind of leadership that drives conversations, throws a curveball in meetings to excite creative thinking, uses your natural voice to get your point across, and advocates for you or your team each time you suddenly stand up to inject some emotion for effect (this latter strategy has an added benefit of creating a pattern interrupt to conditioned thinking). Speaking without apology is managing the perception, not asking for permission. In other words, you care less about what people think and more about why you are qualified to speak your intentions.

Building Executive Presence

Meet Liz, who has maxed out of any further growth in her current role and admittedly has remained there for too long, hoping for a new leadership opportunity. She will not move any higher than where she is nor receive the compensation she knows she's worth. With no more room to grow, Liz has begun looking for a new position elsewhere. She goes on an interview for a new director position. Without any fixed expectations, she focuses on what she knows the role would require and how she could add value. She aces the interview, saying all the right things because she has the skills and work experience behind her to substantiate why she is qualified. Two months later, Liz is sitting behind her new desk as the new director at that company.

Still she finds herself slipping back into old habits that pull her away from a position of authority and power. Just a few weeks into this role, her knee-jerk reaction is to roll up her sleeves and take command without seeking help or feedback from her new team and best resources. She was hired for her strategic eye, the very reason she accepted the role. She also knows what her big-ticket projects are and that she has a lot to learn; yet she struggles, unable to give everything equal priority because she needs more clarity from certain business areas. This affects her self-esteem and, in turn, how she communicates. Seeking to build her success and credibility leaves her unsure if she should jump into speaking without apology while in this honeymoon phase of her career transition. Still trying to assess the lay of the land, she holds back from sharing her honest assessments and what's really on her mind in meetings. She also refrains from asking tough questions too soon. At times, she also judges herself for needing more information before responding to a question or when preparing a presentation. Liz feels frozen and panics, doubting whether she was qualified for this opportunity, and begins to slip into a frame of mind where she believes that she will fail.

Liz has the experience. She has a solid education and a track record that speaks for itself. She was also the company's first choice in its hiring selection, so why would she need to be reassured about her qualifications at this stage? One factor is that in Liz's former senior roles, she always held domain leadership of projects, meaning that she was the sole expert that peers came to for answers and to get things done. In her area of the business, she was a knowledge powerhouse and recognized advisor.

In this new role, she is responsible for new product lines that she has yet to fully understand, and she still needs time to learn everything she needs to know. The good news is that Liz has inherited a team that has been on the ground developing these products and can speak to all the nuances, challenges, and opportunities to get her up to speed quickly.

What Liz is facing is a growth gap, and it will hurt for a short while. Although Liz may initially struggle with finding her voice, it's not because she doesn't believe she's qualified. She doesn't know what she doesn't know *yet*. Company management has placed its trust in her results. By hiring her, the company asked her to design a product vision and then come back and sell it. She is no longer the trusted sage behind the stage who increases others' credibility. To achieve the results she was hired to get and become a leader management can trust, she has to find her voice and create her own platform.

As Liz allows her limiting beliefs to strengthen, her body grows physically weak. This lower energy state will cause a drop in confidence that later can show up as weak language, thereby diluting her value. When she is asked for her opinions and judgment calls, she may say what she needs to say to her audience but later almost falls off her chair when she gets back to her desk because she feels that she has just winged it and once again freezes from panic mode.

Liz initially felt confident that her skills and experience would steer the organization in the right direction. If she were to tap into what she instinctively knows and feels to be solid decisions, her body would strengthen, reinforcing her belief that she will be successful. Without this self-trust in place, Liz can struggle with finding her voice. This lack of confidence and low energy can be picked up by her audience visually through her body language when she leads a meeting or in her emails and aurally via the slight inflections in her dialogue during meetings. If we were on her board of directors, here is how we could help Liz change her mental game.

Liz recognizes that she alone created the opportunity to move into this new executive role. It did not knock on her door blindly. She also knows that she will be the first one in that chair, which felt safe at the time—she knows that she is able to carve out her vision from a blank slate instead of inheriting someone else's grandfathered-in legacy approach. Liz saw this as an opportunity to assess the lay of the land and became enthusiastic at the thought of working in a new market, which inevitably means there would be some time for her to learn the business, going easy on herself. She can also leverage the creative ideas and approach that have always worked for her over her career and simply start there to maintain her confidence. She can focus on having one-on-ones with her constituents and put the right metrics in place to track and communicate progress. This would also support her in building internal relationships—possibly what she identified was lacking in her previous position and therefore a goal she has now committed to. Liz designed the ideal role she wanted, and now here she is with full rein to shape that role how she sees fit, but is she really owning it?

The scenario Liz is facing is no different from what we see when we fail to speak up when we should. We hold back because of some doubt about whether we have anything valuable to add to the conversation, or we defer to those who do. It is a natural tendency to stay put when things are ho-humming smoothly. However, as humans, we cannot survive in such an environment, and this is the very reason Liz left her previous role and accepted this new opportunity.

Once you answer for yourself, "Why am I competent? What do I deliver? To whom?" others begin to see you in that self-started light as well. This is when you are energized and instinctually know that you are ready for more growth. Many midcareer professionals share that they fall back to a humble silence when it comes to speaking up about their work in meetings, even sweeping the questions they need to ask under the rug. Yet these are the experts that are being called on for strategic guidance.

I don't know anyone who has spoken up in a public forum who hasn't been sorry later on because he or she forgot to share a story or piece of information with the audience. Your job is not to have it all figured out. Owning your authority is talking about what you believe, not what you hope would be pleasing to others. Give your clients what they need, but know that this may not always be what they want. As their teacher and resident expert, leading with clarity and intention is how you allay their concerns. When you are clear, they are clear.

Should you ever struggle with second-guessing yourself or questioning whether you have expressed sufficient direction, rest easy. If you felt from your gut at the time that your guidance was sufficient, leaning on ideas that you have found to be effective, then you have given value. You're not there to recite a script; you're there because you are clear on your goal of making an impact, keeping your clients and results at the forefront.

Speaking without apology isn't limited to business relationships. How you show up with your family and friends can make all the difference in how you show up in life. You don't have to be the loudest or the most enthusiastic voice in the room; you just have to trust yourself and how you naturally communicate. You can be soft and direct and still own your authority with quiet power. You can project your voice across a room in a whisper.

Although it can be exciting to take the lead, there's an emotional aspect to being the first one to pitch a vision and lay out a roadmap. It's natural to fear that your recommendations might be rejected. When you have *sold* your services, the next phase is to deliver on those promises and capabilities. As a leader, when you know your product catalog—what you have to offer and whom it would benefit most—your portfolio will speak for itself. Go easy on yourself. This requires face time, where patterns around common themes will appear once you have those much-needed conversations with others.

Before self-sabotage sets in, the truth is that you were not holding up smoke and mirrors when you sold yourself for a position. This is where we tend to freeze and question our self-worth. You were hired to lead, not to blend in and mirror anyone's style. Diversity initiatives in fact encourage the very opposite to drive organization success—attracting people who don't share the same point of view or background. How you naturally lead may not always align with the style of those who brought you in to lead, which will require you to ask, "Am I staying true to my values? Do I own my personal authority?" Go back to your *why*. What does having more leadership mean for you? What does it look like in your new role?

> *The first four or five seconds I tremble every time*
> *I walk out of the wing onto the stage.*
> *Even just going out and looking at the audience*
> *I am terrified for about four seconds, and then it goes away.*
> *I can't explain [it]. I've always had it, all the time.*
> FRANK SINATRA[1]

Speaking in a Group Setting

There's an unspoken dynamic that happens to even the most confident professionals when they speak, and it occurs at the very beginning of a meeting. They experience an inexplicable insecurity and pressure that suddenly weighs them down. This can occur when they kick off a regularly scheduled team meeting, share a quick status, or even switch gears to thank others for their contribution, which would take the attention away from them. They walk away feeling that they hadn't sounded clear and confident enough. They will, however, become more comfortable as the meeting warms up, but from that starting point, there's a bout of anxiety that they don't quite understand. There's a common thread that I have observed in those who struggle with this scenario, including those who have experience with public speaking. They thrive on collaborating in one-on-one conversations versus speaking to a group. They enjoy listening, being supportive, sharing advice, and their topmost priority is to make their colleague feel comfortable. Speaking to a group, however, no matter how large or small, can counter how they are wired when the tendency is to engage naturally through direct contact with one person. They also have more control in navigating a conversation when speaking with someone—not so in a group.

When you're facing a group, whether in person or on a conference call, the spotlight is on you to "perform" on what can feel like a stage, evoking a kind of naked leadership. You may have arrived prepared, and know what you need to say, but there's an intrinsic need to create psychological safety for others in the room without judgment, and for yourself, before you can calmly speak in the room.

Speaking without apology in this scenario is creatively finding ways to speak to a group in a way that feels like a one-on-one conversation. In other words, what can you say that would make you feel as if you are talking to just one individual?

You can share a quick win making small talk with storytelling, which would prompt others to respond and create a chain reaction of lively commentary from a seed you have just planted. You can start with a quick question to an individual asking for his or her feedback about a relevant topic right before you start the agenda. You can put yourself in other people's shoes, tapping into a particular challenge that you are keenly aware these people are facing. You can let them know you have kept the challenge present and plan to circle back to see how you can support them on it. This gesture can also serve as throwing out an olive branch to someone whom others tend to disagree and refrain from collaborating with. You can comment on someone's recent accomplishment. It is likely that another will grab that ball and run with it, echoing the victory across the room with like-minded praise. Should you often need to present, you can pull up a cartoon that mimics how you're feeling today and stir up some light-hearted laughter before jump-starting the agenda. You can open the room with an icebreaker question, turning the focus to the team: "What's new and good? Who wants to share?"

If you're ever unsure of how to calm your nerves before speaking in this type of group interaction, consider what you can say that would feel natural if you were meeting with a favorite client or colleague. Then tweak that commentary that feels like a one-on-one and bring it into a group setting. See how you can tailor and have fun with it, keeping it genuinely you.

Self-Talk Drives Self-Confidence

> *Nobody cares how much you know*
> *until they know how much you care.*
> THEODORE ROOSEVELT

When we address the topic of strong positive dialogue, we must realize that our verbal messages show up in many communication areas. The exchanges we have with others are loud and clear based on how we physically move, how we write our emails, how well we get to the point when sharing something, and even how well we engage a room. Introducing yourself at an intimate work dinner, sharing your best practices, or even telling a joke at an after-hours meetup all lay the groundwork for self-qualifying as someone who communicates well and owns one's value.

Do you want to speak to a larger or more senior audience? Practice with a small group, and build your confidence until you are ready for a larger crowd. Lead a presentation at an industry event where you can leave people thinking, "I liked her ideas. He has a strong message. She knows what she's talking about. I'm going to contact him."

Positive self-talk develops strong physical strength, which improves your confidence and your ability to communicate. Speaking without apology comes from self-awareness and the creation of a self-image that you can own.

"I Can't" or "I Choose Not To"?

Words matter. It is not so much what you say to others but what you say to yourself first. There are certain words you say to yourself that are proved to weaken you, diluting your value and physically causing you to feel powerless. Words such as "I can't" and "I have to" uttered when you are faced with a decision can keep you stuck in the same old routines that, by no coincidence, produce the same old results. In contrast, when we use words such as "I choose *not* to," we recognize that our actions are a direct result of our choices. In other words, you move from a state of powerlessness and lack of control to one where you have free will. Your self-talk gives you the power to choose.

Imagine that you are walking into a room right before you are about to lead a presentation, and assume that you said to yourself, "I will flop and make a fool of myself." Energetically, this self-talk has already projected a negative outcome that likely emanates from your fear of looking foolish. Your body will physically weaken, and you will have created a frequency (energy vibe) of weakness that can be felt even if you say everything perfectly. This is the reason why, when someone is saying all the right things that you want to hear and you're nodding your head in agreement, you still don't feel a sense of trust, although you can't pinpoint why—you just know. The difference between the way you really feel and the affirmation that you're giving by smiling can cause an internal disconnect that weakens you physically. It's much like taking one hand motioning for someone to walk toward you and at the same time using your other hand signaling the person to stop. The juxtaposition of these two actions will cause confusing resistance that weakens you. "I want happiness and success, but don't give it to me right now; I'm not ready." When you're tuned in to your instincts, feel into your body, do you feel uncomfortable? There's no need to question it—you can trust your instincts based on how you feel.

Failure is a self-created negative image that can throw you off balance, causing you to feel frozen. If you can't say everything right, then all bets are off; you have already rejected yourself in advance before anyone has had a chance to. What you say to yourself before you enter a room or start a presentation drives how strong your body feels and hence how powerful your message is. When you show up with rock-solid intention to educate and share from your knowledge store, your listeners will relax, engage, and listen. Standing in a place of anxiety or uncertainty likewise can be absorbed as well, causing your audience to be uneasy or uncomfortable.

Observe the words that you are saying to yourself. Those words matter and will weave their way into every action and decision you make, including how effective you are speaking without apology. In any given situation where you feel an "I can't" inching its way in, such as, "I can't get through this day after that painfully long commute," step on the brakes and stop. Whenever you give your mind a limiting belief to feed on, which translates to an "I can't," you are automatically lying. In truth, there's nothing you cannot try to accomplish. Carefully observe the words you are saying to yourself because they can become thought patterns that are locked in as truth—your truth. At this stage, they can become so ingrained that they serve as a distortion, holding you back from claiming your personal authority.

Self-doubt moves you out of integrity every time and can stem from many factors—suffering from a lack of focus or not enough sleep, being in a loud or toxic environment, or even telling a white lie. When you are not standing in integrity, your body weakens. When your body weakens, your muscles physically go limp. When your muscles go limp, your energy and confidence levels follow suit and take a plunge as well. This downward spiral results in weak language that can cause you to become unfocused and lose clarity on what you originally intended to say.

Release Limiting Beliefs

I can't lead a global team.
I can't lead professionals who are older than I am.
I can't ask for additional compensation.

There are many flavors of self-doubt. It can rear its head in an action, and rationally, you may already know that its message is untrue. However, this is not what's important. The more relevant question is, "Are you always projecting that you are good enough?" Language plays a significant role here. By making subtle tweaks to your internal dialogue, you can quickly own any conversation so that there isn't any doubt in anyone's mind, especially your own, about your commitment and intention.

Achieving the things that you want in your life begins with eliminating all doubt. Think of a desire as no more than an energy wave. When you allow self-doubt in, it too has a frequency, only in the opposite direction of your desire. Therefore, two opposing intentions inevitably will cancel each other out energetically. An example of this is when you see a rainbow effect from a film of oil floating on water. The waves reflected from both the inside and outside surface will interfere with one another, cancel out white light, and therefore result in color. Being aware of your thoughts, and whether they are producing positive or negative signals, is why being intentional is fundamental to speaking *and* feeling unapologetic.

Suppose that you have always dreamed of relocating to a warmer climate. One day, you say, "I will move to a new home where I can enjoy endless sunshine." A few days pass, and the self-doubt begins to creep in. Loved ones start to wave your pipedream away with a chuckle. Essentially, you have allowed your environment in and just erased creating what you want.

After you've had some time to consider whether your goal is a possibility, you don't feel as prepared to uproot your family or perhaps risk losing your well-paying position through relocation. Your initial desire, filled with childlike enthusiasm, never stood a chance of gaining momentum because it was swiftly erased from your belief system due in part to your environment and possibly any other number of factors you may have allowed in.

You don't have to work hard at everything you want as much as you have to eliminate resistance to what you want and believe that those things are possible and why you deserve to receive them. Creating positive images of what you want accelerates your beliefs. Through repetition, you affirm your beliefs as statements until they become locked in your mind as truth: "I am buying that home," "I am finding my life partner," or "I enjoy a flexible schedule so that I can spend more time with my family."

You swap self-doubt with positive expectation. Sabotaging beliefs will physically weaken you every time and can cause you to show up with weak language. Positive affirmations, in contrast, replace negative thoughts with expected outcomes that develop your sea legs, giving your desires breathing room and strengthening your courage to persevere.

When you create your mental fertile ground, you set up any corner of your life for success and growth. Whatever you ask for shows up in the form of opportunities, people, and resources to support you. Owning your authority is developing an instinctive belief in what you have the potential to create until it materializes into your life. This can't happen until you lose your limiting beliefs, and this is why pushing hard doesn't work. When you release the dam of disbelief, you step into your greatest potential by putting yourself in a state of steady flow. It's why doors suddenly start to fly open when you begin to feel light and carefree. You're not fixated on any outcome, but are committed to enjoying the ride with some skin in the game and betting on you.

LISTENING WITHOUT APOLOGY

You won't find a more priceless listening skill to support you than when you can break barriers being formed in your organization, through diplomacy. This is where you observe communication channels shut down between divisions or functional areas, conflicts rising from hard feelings, or special interests and policies being misunderstood. Diplomatic leadership requires having awareness and sharp listening skills to assist your constituents where needed. When you listen without apology, you effectively equip yourself to resolve communication gaps. You also create a culture of diplomats who can see a colleague that's fixated on a specific strategy and step in to help him or her to take another approach to achieve their vision. Support can come in the form of advising on the next steps to "push things along" or aiding in prioritizing the more impactful activities to support the greater good.

In order for you to drive change, you have to pinpoint where change is needed—that's your impact opportunity. This can involve sitting down with an internal client to improve his or her current process, working with a leadership team to support a restructure, or even at home helping an overwhelmed child with his or her studies so as to make the grade.

You can implement change simply by having a highly tuned ear that recognizes the strains between business units and then discovering how you can bridge those gaps. You can learn about the systems and processes that are on life support or that suffer from inefficiencies that need to be addressed and ultimately retired to make way for new workflows.

Let's go back to fearless Liz, who is leading a lucrative product line at her company. Her work depends on countless algorithms that are baked into the products that she's responsible for. Does she know the inner workings of every product that is most profitable? No. Would it be valuable for her to understand how everything works internally? Absolutely, but probably not practical or necessary in her role. As an active listener, she discovers a disconnect between the product engineers and the business that can potentially result in a halt in work progress. Liz reaches out and asks how she could support the team that is doing the product design. She learns what the challenges are and takes that back to the business audience. She not only bridges the communication gap with the nontechnical audience but also increases her market value by being an advocate for engineers and speaking their language. She unapologetically takes down the human-created silos and gets momentum building again through collaboration.

By taking responsibility for communication voids, instinctively feeling out what others need, you influence change and earn trust in your key business relationships. By taking on natural listening skills, you facilitate the flow of crucial information that helps others do their jobs better.

It's not a struggle to voice your thoughts so much as it is to see yourself as a single point of influence. The disconnect lies in feeling qualified to speak your expertise but not always homing in on your personal power to influence change.

We are more likely to speak up in a room full of people who would likely agree with us than sticking our necks out too much and risking looking foolish. Remember that your job is not to please everyone. People don't need to like you; they just need to respect what you have to share. Abrasive leadership, in contrast, needs to control a conversation.

Often the perceived strength in business communication lies in speaking over listening; yet being a good listener is a core strength that helps you help your clients with what they are trying to achieve. Listening shows that you have a keen understanding of their roadblocks so that you can make that phone call to push things along and "bridge" with others, calmly stating the circumstances that require support. Listening also helps you relate to others naturally because that's how you are wired. Listening is not something you need to learn; you were born listening. Lean into this skill as much as you can to strengthen it so that others feel they are being heard and are being given the attention they deserve. If you tend to be reserved, be aware of the risk of being seen as too quietly cautious, which may instill a lack of trust in others, which, in turn, may cause them to develop a lack of trust in you.

Filter Out the Noise

Speaking without apology is also being a sounding board by filtering out the noise when you are being flooded with a surge of information from possibly poor leadership. In any meeting, you can crystallize the priorities for the team that are being conveyed, which can mobilize people toward a better understood campaign. In this scenario, you can step back and mentally throw out all the topics that are irrelevant from the discussion and ensure that everyone is clear on next steps. Focus only on the things you believe to be meaningful by leading with the following:

> *"Let us test our understanding. Here's what we heard you say..."*
>
> *"Here's what we will focus on..."*
>
> *"Let's recap the agreements and make sure that we're all on the same page..."*

Regurgitate what you understood by recapping the takeaways to ensure that everyone is aligned. When there is radio silence, people may assume that you've understood and are in full agreement. However, by taking the time to filter out the noise before the meeting closes, you protect your team. This should put people at ease, or trigger a call for more clarity and everyone can walk away with consensus.

Blind Spots

Being present in a meeting, hearing the priorities and agenda, under-standing the challenges and potential roadblocks, and chiming in with an opinion are all ways you can be impactful as a decision maker. How can you authentically also own your authority by sharing valid concerns based on your instincts? You can shift from waiting for permission to turning on a radar for what's not being talked about. Through examination of those blind spots that should be escalated, you can determine who on the team can step up and take on more respon-sibility, leveraging their opportunity to grow. Following one's instincts is a skill that new leaders particularly struggle with when they are pro-moted based on merit instead of seniority, and feel subject to greater criticism, yet will be their best strategy to build trust over time.

Speaking without apology is going against the grain when your opinion is likely to be the only one that points out the elephant in the room. It's throwing out an idea that no one else has considered and either taking the risk of being the lone ranger, thereby isolating yourself, or enjoying a string of high-fives for being so innovative. You elevate yourself in small increments by picking up the phone and say-ing, "I heard about the pushed-up deadline. Here are the risks, and more important, here's how we can support you."

By not speaking up and not pointing out risks, your own reputa-tion can be on the line, and you may be perceived as someone who is afraid to act. You may not have all the answers, but insight is never an exact science. Instinctively, you may see the blinking yellow alerts and feel an impulse to act—to act on instinct. If you were to look back at the decisions you've made in your life that didn't turn out well, did your gut always know the truth?

James was never comfortable being the one to press "code red" whenever a snafu surfaced on a project that would affect his team's timeline. He didn't want his group to be the messenger of bad news or challenge another team's poor leadership that may have been responsible. He is tied to a likability trait. It would be a bold move for him to speak up, accept scrutiny, and stir up potential conflict. And yet, acting in full integrity, if you know that you have caught a major issue before it goes into a tailspin, you are taking responsibility as a leader. There's also a direct cost to remaining silent. The choice to say and do nothing could hurt a project later on, and you could quickly lose credibility.

If you maintain radio silence, you are seen as not caring enough about the organization, protecting your reputation first by not raising the yellow flags. Here's how I've often seen the harsh backlash that results from not speaking up: key decision makers get dinged in meetings. "So James, did you not think that looming iceberg you knew about weeks ago was relevant enough to share with the rest of us?"

Was it James's intention to sweep critical information under the rug? That was probably not his intention. When people don't feel that they have the power to do anything about a problem because it doesn't fall under their direct domain or responsibility, they tend to let it fall and turn a blind eye. Speaking without apology is going from "not on my watch" to acting in spite of and sounding the alarm for all who can be affected.

All Feedback Is Good Feedback

You may not always like it or secretly wish that you could avoid it, but if you're not seeking feedback on a regular basis, you are missing out on a crucial opportunity to expand your growth as a leader. Feedback gives you the focus you need so that you can improve your performance over time.

As children, when we were just developing and learning how to acquire our sense of self, we looked to our parents or guardians as our primary source of feedback to shape our behavior. This early relationship was the key to helping us feel capable, competent, and loved.

As adults, some of us have acquired a knee-jerk reaction to feedback as criticism, even if it has the potential to point us in a better direction, saving time we would have otherwise lost. The benefit of leaning into feedback—whether it comes from a difficult colleague, someone with higher authority, or even a past client—is that you can always learn from it. You learn to respond differently to certain personalities, environments, and circumstances. By embracing raw, honest conversations, you can become desensitized to critical feedback, which allows you to step back and process the message without self-judgment. Leaders who speak without apology seek feedback and also solicit opinions from their teams in order to see their own blind spots.

Leading by example, giving others feedback for a job well done, and encouraging your team to speak up for themselves all establish a sense of trust and inclusion. Even the most prominent leaders can fail to listen to others' opinions, which they so desperately should rely on.

Cultural Inclusion Is Feedback

*How successful you are, is based on how
included you make people feel in the room.*

If you consider your team a "work family," how would you say that your team members are engaged? Diversity and inclusion programs place an inclusion metric at the forefront of the strategic agenda, but it's not only an equity and inclusion issue. Engagement starts at the top of an organization's leadership and trickles down, driving how work cultures form and, ultimately, how employees learn to "play together." When employees don't feel visible, are bored, or consider themselves passive members of the family, certain patterns become evident and are easily quantifiable. The classic scene where this becomes most apparent is in the routine daily meeting. Do you see most employees acting like invited guests, or are they self-qualifying to lead by speaking up as hosts of the meeting even if they did not set the agenda?

Put yourself in the shoes of an invited guest at an evening event. Invited guests typically sit back, observe, and listen. They walk into a room for the first time, assess the company they are in, and aren't really sure of the protocol. They will wait to be asked if they want a drink or wish to sit down. They will spend their time fitting in, smiling, and nodding their heads, and they often speak only when spoken to, until they gain a comfort level in the room.

In contrast, if they feel like a host, they take ownership of the room. They are firmly seated at the table, not on the sidelines, taking a backseat or borrowing someone else's chair. They check to see if everyone has a drink and is comfortable. They chat freely to see how everyone's weekend was and if there's anything that someone wants to share with the group. They share their opinions and ideas and encourage others to do the same. They believe that their thoughts matter. They consider themselves a vital part of the family operation and a stakeholder in ensuring that the rest of the night runs like a well-oiled machine.

When you change your frame of mind from feeling like an invited guest to feeling like you are the host, that's when you should expect to instinctively speak up by:

Taking more ownership
Making greater contributions
Sharing more of your expert judgment
Feeling more confident
Taking on more risk
Making more decisions
Sharing a million-dollar idea

Leaders who pay attention to the level of inclusion at their organization ask their employees such questions as:

"Do you feel that you have a place at the table?"

"Do you feel that your input and opinions are sought after?"

"Do you feel valued for your background, experience, and unique views?"

The feedback from these questions and the frequency with which your employees see others speaking without apology lay the groundwork for change. Historically, corporations have not been seen as places where people are encouraged to speak openly, and yet emotion is what drives consumers to buy their products. Speak to your product, not to the process. People don't buy into processes and best practices. They buy into results based on how emotionally moved they are when they make a purchase. Likewise, they buy into you as their trusted resource to help them reach their desired result—your work product on which you have built your reputation.

SHHHHH . . . *SILENT* SPELLS THE WORD *LISTEN*

When we think about being good communicators, we often focus on what we should say and do to get our message across. We don't always give much weight to the message we send by remaining silent. This sounds somewhat contradictory. How can we own our authority and speak powerfully while saying nothing? When you find yourself in a discussion that is spiraling in another direction, going silent can be an instinctive strategy to save and win back the focus that you need. You can use it when you are losing buy-in or during any form of negotiation. Emotions can run so high that you can easily snap back in frustration. By disengaging, you can take back the conversation and return to why you are there in the first place, using a tactical tool called the *pregnant pause.*

Say more by saying less. The pregnant pause is when you *stop.* You stop talking. You have made your points, outlining your position. You lean back in your chair, visibly demonstrating that you are listening intently. If you are on the phone, you can take a long, deep breath and allow an incredibly awkward moment of silence to float across the wire. Creating an uncomfortable environment is the point of this technique. This gives the other person the time to process the information you just shared and consider a solution that works for both of you to fill the awkward space. While you can never tell what wheels will start turning, when you use this tactic, the person to whom you are talking will quickly become aware of your solid position.

This mini timeout takes back your power on several levels. You avoid going into reactive mode, which can leave you feeling desperate to win the other person to your side. With quiet power, you demonstrate that you do not need to respond to everything asked of you or justify your position, which squarely puts you back in control of the conversation. This is also an effective strategy to encourage others to speak, which buys you more time to work on your response. By pausing, you also allow your last words to resonate longer and make a stronger impact. Silence, in this case, becomes your best tool and can turn a conversation around quickly in your favor.

> Insurance agent Juan trains his sales team in the office on how to speak to customers who inquire about better premiums on their policies. "I tell my people to listen to what the client wants, take their time to crunch the numbers, and then come back and calmly lay out all the options that are possible: 'I can offer you this option or this option. This is what I can do, and this is what I can't do.' Then I instruct them to stop talking. As salespeople, we're almost wired with loose lips to keep talking and win the customer, but that doesn't work in this situation. People tune out the salesperson shtick when they have one objective on their minds. By injecting silence into the air, we put the ball squarely in their court with all the information they need to make a decision. If they choose to stay on as our client or go, either way, it's fine. We did everything we could to paint the picture they asked for and spell out the possibilities. The only

thing you can do is let go, and taking a pregnant pause is a huge driver of that process."

This uncomfortable pause can be used when you are asked a question you don't feel you or your team needs to respond to. You stop talking and let silence and tension rise across the room.

Here's how you can effectively use the pregnant pause: if this is an in-person meeting, make direct eye contact while showing consideration for the other person's thoughts. As a mindful professional, this is where you thrive. You are most comfortable when you listen and process, and this not only will calm you but also will give you time to consider all your options.

The pregnant pause is a powerful technique that you can use in interviews, one-on-one meetings, negotiations, or any conversation where you need to communicate or ask for something that will support your efforts. Can you visualize the power of the pregnant pause when negotiating the purchase of a new car? You can reserve this technique for discussions in which you instinctively expect to receive pushback. Taking a pregnant pause can also be effective when you are leading a group, following the flow of energy in a room, when you open the room up for questions and insights allowing attendees to be visible and find their voice from raising their hand. Words speak volumes when you say less.

There are five typical scenarios where professionals can go into freeze mode at work:

- When they are overwhelmed by a project workload that has competing priorities
- When they fear making a mistake
- When they fear looking foolish from making a poor decision
- When they experience interpersonal conflict with a colleague or superior
- When they are put on the spot by a curveball question to which they don't immediately have an answer

For the highly organized, this last scenario can hurt more if you are suddenly caught off guard while speaking to a large room. Let go, and throw out the preplanned script. To hold the line and navigate this scenario without feeling foolish, *listen.*

As noted above, the word *silent* contains the same letters as the word *listen.* No rule book says that you need to respond right away. Speaking without apology can also mean going silent. Take that pregnant pause and buy yourself some time, embrace your instincts, and reassure your audience that you are listening. Speak slowly and step-by-step. We've all been around those who go around answering a question without giving a simple response.

GET TO THE POINT

Whenever you're feeling under pressure to make a timeline, you may appreciate that those who seek your attention are able to do one particular thing well—they know how to get to the point. When you are on the other side of the table and speaking with someone when time is limited, you may feel rushed and a sense of being closed off, which can affect how you communicate and your overall confidence level.

You can easily lose your intention when you sense that another party is not listening. You are likely not imagining it. This is the time to turn the dial to the other person's channel. Consider why the person would want to listen to what you have to say. Are you speaking the person's language? Are you clear on the fact that what you are advising will matter to him or her, not you?

Getting to the point is painting a clear picture with a message that conveys, "Here's where we are, and here's where we need to be." Don't go too deep or you will lose your listeners. Roll it up for them, and avoid diving into too many details. The more you can get into your clients' shoes, the more reception and airtime you will receive. When you make your message more about them and less about you, you become relatable, and they will give you two seconds more of their time.

I also invite you to consider the mini battles that your managers or clients are facing from their corner of the world. Unbeknown to you, there may be sirens going off in their heads before your arrival. A low attention span can have absolutely nothing to do with you. The only question racing in their minds when you sit down can be, "Should I engage, or should I reschedule for another time?"

Now there you are walking into the room, fully intending to highlight key issues and concerns that need to be dealt with. There's always the possibility that you can naturally rub someone the wrong way or work for someone with zero emotional intelligence. This is beyond your control. A stirred-up sense of job insecurity, overwhelm, peer-to-peer rivalry, or unconscious bias—any one of these—can create resistance between you and a client or someone in a position of authority through no fault of your own. If your intention remains to continue to do your job well and you're not going anywhere anytime soon, I strongly encourage you to speak without apology by getting to the point at every opportunity. Park any emotion at the door, focus on the business goals, and authentically lead from a place that feels comfortable while keeping meetings as time efficient as possible. This should free you up to do more of what you enjoy in your role and allow you to stay true to your beliefs by owning your authority.

The Rule of Three

You can't speak without apology and engage your audience without applying the *rule of three* in some way. This is a powerful communication strategy in which you take all the information you want to discuss and shorten it down to three bullet points, flowing with a 1-2-3 rhythm that your listener can follow. Whether you need to brief someone on an important update or require a decision to be made, speaking less is always more and is why this rule is so effective. People don't want to be snowed in by too much information at once. You speak without apology when you can keep it short and get to the relevant topics that will command attention, leading from your perspective.

You can appreciate the power of the rule of three when you're on the receiving end, watching (with eyes glazed over) someone lead a presentation that typically would take 10 minutes and yet stretches to an hour because of the influx of too much information. Implementing the rule of three demonstrates that you respect your audience's time because you focus only on what those people need to know. Ideally, you want to convey just enough information to help them make a decision, once again filtering out the noise. On the speaking circuit, we see the rule of three at play in every keynote presentation or talk. Listen closely, and you will hear the speaker highlighting three takeaways, three benefits, three examples, or three personal stories to grab your attention.

Another ideal opportunity to use this approach is right before a meeting or conference call ends. You quickly recap the conversation, summarizing what everyone agreed to, identifying the next steps needed to move forward, and locking it in by focusing on the key points of view.

BEING BEFORE SPEAKING

Words matter, but your dialogue isn't limited to verbal language. Your primary form of communicating is always through intention. The intention you set for those tuning in to you. People will feel your meaning and energy without you ever having to say a word. When you can embrace that others are following their instincts when they are listening to, watching, or reading you, there's less of a need to be concerned about what you should say—allow your personality to shine through when you speak your intentions. This empowers you to let go and feel lighter and more playful in every exchange.

What can you share to help your clients feel understood by you? What repeating patterns have been coming up that your clients need support on right now?

Be good to yourself: set out to create collaborative discussions in which you can place a few client concerns in your hip pocket, support your clients in getting in the game, and establish trust. If you are funny, bring humor into the room. If you are smart and witty, bring that energy with full force. Tune into social cues or drop a quick line about an interesting article you just read. Powerful dialogue is simply sharing what you know in your own authentic way.

Often people just want to pick your brain and learn your opinions on a subject, not expecting anything more from you. If you are asked for your opinion, talk about what you believe and how things can be done better. Speaking without apology is mentally finishing each sentence with "Here's what I know" and owning your power by letting go. At this stage, your job is to listen: listen to what's coming up for your clients, leading from their corner of the business, and listen to how you can help and create new opportunities that can influence change.

When Oprah Winfrey began her television broadcasting career, she tried on Barbara Walters' personality because of her deep admiration. At the time, Walters was the only accomplished female journalist and role model in the broadcasting industry. Pinning Barbara Walters' personality on top of Oprah's, however, didn't flow very well to viewers. It wasn't until Oprah embraced her own voice on screen that the floodgates opened and the world discovered Oprah.

Engage your authentic voice everywhere. You know what feels and sounds right, and you also know what needs to be said when the room has gone silent. You can endeavor to keep others accountable, or you can disagree with the popular opinion in the room. The more you become comfortable with your words that hold meaning, the easier it becomes to speak without apology. Hold firm to your belief that your message has meaning. It's uncomfortable to get comfortable with expressing yourself naturally and detached from what others may want to hear. Nonetheless, you can practice this until you own your message and exercise a muscle that's sourced from intention.

Nodding your head to gain approval will always feel more comfortable than raising your hand to object. Once in a while, a need to please can hold you back from your genuine voice. Embrace the discomfort of a potential conflict and speak up anyway despite any fear you may have.

Your voice is heard everywhere—through the way you write your emails, the clothing that you wear, and even your body language when you walk across a room. How do you enter a conversation? How do you listen? These are all communication methods that tell a story about who you are, and others can feel it. The more self-aware you are, the more present you are to others in the room.

When I moved from the buy to the sell side of Wall Street, my jaw dropped the moment I stepped onto the trading floor. Everyone was dressed to attend what felt like a summer barbeque. I wasn't clutching my pearls, but I did notice an immediate drop in my energy level. I felt out of place at once, given the sharp contrast presented by the formal gray suit I had worn that day. I had two options to blend in: I could either wing it by sticking to my preferred professional dress code or adapt to everyone else.

Stepping into uncomfortable territory, I decided to try on jeans and a t-shirt one day, and I immediately felt a swift change in my body, followed by a drop in my communication. It would have been easy to change my wardrobe to fit in with everyone, but I would not have felt as confident. I chose to keep it real with suits that aligned authentically with who I was. That experience taught me how important it is to align with your personal style of dress, because it drives how well you communicate.

There will always be days when you lose your mojo and feel thoroughly ungrounded. You could have started off the morning on a wrong note, hit traffic, or missed the alarm. Now there you are walking through the door, showing up less confident and with weak language. You can try to sweep it under the rug. You may take the calls you need to and show up at meetings, but are you fully present? Work responsibilities or other distractions can quickly pull you in, causing you to be there in body but not necessarily in spirit.

A quick and easy indicator of knowing how your language may be weakening you is to notice how others are responding to you. Are they steering clear? Are they cherry-picking their words with you? Are you receiving fewer drop-ins and emails than usual? If, for example, you notice that you are being pulled into conversations in which there is an overall negative vibe, it's time to take a step back and look within. This is self-leadership. How did you feel that day? Did your day begin on a positive note? Were you feeling less confident? Go easy on yourself. A quick way to recalibrate and step back into your skin is to decide how you want to feel throughout the remainder of the day.

The following is an exercise you can do whenever you feel off-balance or in a state of resignation. It's also a great way to quickly regain focus and raise your energy level to prepare for any upcoming presentation, meeting, or discussion, remaining intentional to how you want to feel. This technique is also used by singers to chamber airflow and is proved to raise your confidence level because you are pacing yourself to create inner calm.

- Find a comfortable chair and a private space.
- Cross your ankles and forearms.
- Close your eyes, and center your focus on your abdomen. With shoulders relaxed, allow your rib cage to rest.
- Imagine a bright shining light at the center of your stomach.
- Take a deep belly breath in from your nose. Hold it for a few seconds, and slowly exhale from your mouth. Then repeat. On each exhale, imagine the light at your core is getting brighter.
- Close your eyes, and take 10 deep breaths, once more in through the nose and out through the mouth. Count backward 10, 9, 8 on the inhale and slowly exhale on 7, 6, 5, 4, 3, 2, 1.
- Repeat again, counting backward. Repeat counting until you feel grounded and your body strengthened.

This breathing exercise increases oxygen to the brain and cells in your body, which will give you the boost you need to raise your energy and confidence.

When you are done, open your eyes. What is your intention in the upcoming meeting, phone conversation, or interview? Focus on only one thing you want to create—only one. What do you visualize as the person's response to what you share? Whatever comes up from your gut at the end of this exercise was not random. Embrace your instincts, create a segment of engagement in your mind, and imagine how it will flow. Now let it go. You are right where you need to be. Your body, now centered and self-calibrated, will know what to do. Speak intentional affirmations silently in your mind: "I am clear on my value. I am confidently speaking. My opinions are being heard."

You should observe a clearing of mind from this exercise or from any experience where you can shut out the noise and the ego that otherwise would have free rein to prevent you from speaking with ease. When you go about your daily routine, your focus tends to be on experiences that you pull from your five senses. Yet that sixth sense—your instinct—is where your playing field lives and how you can design new experiences—through your thoughts, actions, and images of your future. This is what you fully expect to happen, positively or negatively.

SMALL TALK AND STORYTELLING

From the beginning of human civilization, storytelling has been the communication vehicle that builds trust between people, helping them relate to one another and understand where they stand in the context of their environment. Today, this form of engagement still holds great authority, universally connecting and bonding us based on our common personal experiences. Stories also speak a universal language that builds camaraderie and fun into conversation. You don't have to be a brilliant storyteller or even tell good jokes. You just have to be willing to go with your gut and jump in with a quick story every once in a while.

Many leaders share that they are unsure of how effective they are at storytelling and making small talk and easily overlook those stories as the tools of confidence and influence that they truly are. You start when it feels right and it doesn't feel like you're trying too hard.

From a quick story, you can share a clear and concise message that can influence others to buy in to your perspective so that you can pitch your vision more creatively. The primary rule of thumb of storytelling is to do one thing: answer why others should care. In other words, how does what you are sharing make a difference and impact them? Gain a bird's-eye view of their world, and you will find what to say based on what's relevant to them, not you.

Also, be mindful of different leadership styles. Some people need time to warm up before a meeting and before they will embrace any new idea. When you sit down with them, you'll find that they enjoy cozy chitchat before talking shop. Others, in contrast, may like to dig into business right away, and some can frown on jumping straight into work, especially if it's on a Monday, and would prefer to connect through a lively weekend recap. You will adjust to storytelling by knowing your audience and when it feels right to dive right into business. Others will notice and appreciate this about you.

In Japanese culture, there's an unspoken rule that while you don't have to wait for permission to sit down, you also don't want to be the only one sitting. If your Japanese hosts are sitting, then you will not be the one to break the ice. This applies to any group interaction: a meeting, talk, drinks gathering, or company dinner. Speaking without apology is being mindful of and adapting to others' styles and instinctively feeling when it's the best time to switch to sharing a story.

As a former technology leader responsible for delivering data, I have recognized that information itself does not inspire people. Although information is a vital part of decision making, it often feels too dry. Good leaders rest their credibility on using data and metrics, but they know that storytelling around those numbers is what builds trust. Consider the documents you present and the stories you can easily tell about them, clearly sharing a single message.

Storytelling is no more than rolling up all the information you want to convey into a simple story. No one wants to read the 10-bullet slide presentation. Walk your listeners through it and take them out of the weeds with a story that draws out your vision. Wrap a compelling picture around information that would otherwise feel dull and lifeless. You can quickly take people from chaos to calm by allowing your stories to take the lead and drive your message home.

When you are unsure of where to start, consider the perspective of others and how the world looks through their lens, putting yourself in their shoes. What would make the most sense for those people to know, and what is relevant right now? Trusting your instincts is being relevant and timely with what you share, when, and with whom.

Another effective technique in creating small talk that feels natural is to paint before and after pictures for your listeners. What does the world look like before and after your ideas, recommendations, or directives? When you speak to any size audience, whether on a conference call or in person, weave in the before and after pictures as you see them. This showcases your value by walking your listeners through what the current state is and then fast-forwarding to the results you promise through your leadership—and ultimately what they stand to gain.

As an expert in the organization, it's your responsibility to educate your team and managers on the current pain points and challenges. Then draw out what improvements and solutions look like given the collective best recommendations of your team. Now you can swiftly engage with those takeaways and work backward so that you don't lose them, showing what that future state looks like. Why would the people in your audience care to listen? Turn the focus around; dedicate it to them. Start with a story, and lead into why they would benefit.

CALLS TO ACTION

In every conversation that you lead, whether in emails, a phone call, or a presentation, you are always leaving your audience with some call to action. You could be leading your clients to a course correction after you have spent 15 minutes highlighting the pitfalls their team is unknowingly making. Calls to action also show up each time you secure buy-in and before you close, confirming the action to be taken that will move the agenda along. Writing intuitive subject lines to your team emails using words such as "Next Steps" is a powerful way to guide them so that they know what they are being called to focus on and how they can respond. Recapping roles and responsibilities, stating your ask at the beginning of an email, and highlighting people's names throughout your message all influence your readers to scroll down and keep reading further to ensure that you have their attention and can mobilize them to take some form of action.

You also discover your call to action when you need to push back on others who may unknowingly encroach on your time. Freely pointing them to someone who can help is your call to action that protects your best time and energy. It's also ending with a commitment whenever you close a meeting, where everyone involved understands what they need to do next to push ahead, and there are no loose ends. Calls to action instill a sense of urgency and priority to maintain productivity and momentum.

The secret to influencing others to act is always in the follow-up and something many leaders leave on the table or struggle with communicating effectively. The risk to not closing with a call to action and securing follow-up is missed deadlines that can be dropped or high-priority projects that fall by the wayside. Without a follow-up, lines of communication can also go radio silent. Unfortunately, when too much time passes, following up can morph into putting you in a position where you must chase others down. This can be avoided if you set as a best practice for your team to create clear calls to action to save everyone time from chasing the follow-up.

Speaking without apology creates an experience where others feel understood by you and motivated into action after your brief time together. Plant the seed of an idea for your team. Educate them. Give them some quick tools to improve something they can run with and "plus" them into creating positive change. When you are a go-giver, you go from the professional they came to sit with for a half hour to the expert they can have in their hip pocket and take home with them. Whether you write an email, have lunch, speak on stage, give a presentation, or have a phone exchange, as a leader, your job is to create an experience (including with your own team) that encourages an expansion of ideas and creative thinking.

Let your personality shine through in your language. Words matter and will land more powerfully when they evoke an upbeat, positive message that speaks of progress and movement.

Turning this around, how do you feel when you are waiting for a call to action? Hanging out on the bench, waiting around for you or your team to be picked, can make you feel powerless and will not support your goals energetically. Is there a pattern of taking a "wait-and-see" approach in any area of your life? Notice how you feel when you set an intention to be placed on someone's calendar and then effectively lock it in, no longer accepting *no* or waiting for a response.

Subtle tweaks in how you communicate on a daily basis can strengthen the weak language that may be diluting you. What is the conversation, presentation, meeting, or interview that you need to create to gain your next career breakthrough? Listen to your gut, and commit verbally to something that you wouldn't normally commit to that will help you grow. Tap into anything that evokes an instinctual nudge. Circle in this book anything that you are not doing, and write anything that you should be doing instead. Remove your inner critic; this exercise is not meant to discourage. If anything you write down is an instinctive flag you feel would improve your leadership skills, it is valuable feedback to support your career success because it is sourced from your gut.

What is something that you can do after reading this book? What can you do right now to start small that will build your confidence and strengthen your instincts? Look at something that you have been avoiding, and commit to one simple action you can take now. This is how you begin owning your personal authority and designing a career (and life) that you love.

6

HONING YOUR INTUITION

SHARPENING IT

During the week of March 9, 2020, the top trend of queries punched into Google in the United States showed a spike in the search terms "meditation" and "mindfulness," which would last for weeks to come. The World Health Organization had just officially announced a global pandemic. People were faced with a dire situation they felt powerless to control, and so the collective instinctual response was to turn to tools that deliver calm in a state of uncertainty and imminent chaos.

Mastering your mental game is not a new concept. In sports, it is the core muscle that any successful athlete flexes before working his or her physical game. It's used anywhere from improving your golf swing to dealing with financial burdens that come into your life. Intuition, however, has never been as mainstream outside of spiritual and New Age thinking. The idea that intuition is a major component of learning and self-development was never part of our schooling because it hasn't been proved and built on any scientific evidence. As children, we were never taught to act on our impulses. Intuitive inspiration is not a channel most people consciously tune into, and yet intuition produces the very thoughts that nudge us to call the person who can take our career or business to the next level, help us to meet our life partner, or allow us to find that ideal new home we have only dreamt of. It's also the primary channel through which we develop trust in ourselves.

As a leader in any area of your life (finances, health, family, career), you have to be willing to follow your instincts. You have to be willing to lead from that inner voice. You have to be ready to bank on you, driven by the conviction that you know who you are and why you are here on this planet—your purpose. Perhaps you have never verbalized your purpose or are unsure of what that is. Should that be so, there is another truth in that statement. You always know when it's *not* present and when you don't feel connected in an area of your life. This realization will inevitably draw you closer to discovering what *does* fulfill you and what you would feel passionate about. There is one caveat, however. Finding your purpose doesn't come from a logical deduction. This is pure heart-driven self-leadership where you allow your values to guide you.

What if you mentally prepared for difficult circumstances before they happened, including taking on small levels of risk by acting on things that would make you uncomfortable and possibly even unprepared for? Do you subscribe to the belief that through the power of your mind, you can design a life where you can thrive, not just survive?

When you examine your thought patterns and the filters through which you interpret the world, you are thought to be living consciously. You are in a state of being with the very things that are aligned with your values and what's important to you versus making choices that are never vetted to see if they will make you happy. Intuition helps you to stay the course, where any decision you make is lined up from your internal compass and is the very thing that will make you grow. How often you follow your instincts is directly related to how much you believe in yourself, and this drives your confidence level and the level of risk you are willing to take in all areas of your life, not just your career.

Intuition is your ability to feel something suddenly without any logical explanation. It's the feeling that influences you, rather than the inclination to yield to external pressure or circumstances. This is not to say that you should lead your life on a wing and a prayer; the idea is to become more aware of the point of focus of your thoughts and what you're being guided toward. It's also to lean on past success patterns and identify when you can rely on decisions that hold similar characteristics.

An intuitive hit is a random thought that you suddenly have when there is no particular person, conversation, or event in your frame of reference. These thoughts often arrive when you are taking a shower, getting dressed, cleaning, or doing the dishes—any mindless activity that creates a blank canvas in your mind. That's the only fertile ground you need. You know when an intuitive impulse occurs. You can feel it. You suddenly stop, straighten your back, and pay close attention without question. The unexpected intrusion alone makes you take notice and causes you to be reluctant to wave it away as nonsense, even though it violates the principles of logic.

When you experience such instinctive impulses, give them the focus they are quietly screaming for. Pause and ask if there is any action you can take at that moment that feels possible and offers no resistance? Don't question it. Take that next step and press "Go." There's a reason why your instinct is leading you there and why immediate action is so essential. When you wait too long, the feeling fades, and you rationalize away your initial impulse, never following up with any action. What's important to note is that the energy field that swept up to surround and support you is never the same hours later, and this is why it's crucial to act quickly when it feels right. You may not be able to explain your decision to anyone even if you want to. You just know.

When you are in any difficult or challenging circumstance, asking for a solution, the answer typically never arrives on cue, in that moment. Here are some ways you can accelerate the process:

- Engage in activities that make you feel light, playful, and carefree.
- Notice nonverbal cues. These can be in the form of an impulse, sign, or subtle message aligned with what your thoughts are focused on.

- Jump into a random yet timely conversation with someone who offers support.
- Flex a creative muscle through writing, cooking, or drawing; this is when you are at your highest energy state to increase your intuition.
- Find calm spaces that help quiet your mind. These are environments where you can meditate, listen to relaxing music or white noise, do yoga, or enjoy nature.
- Be of service to someone; offer your time and support.

Letting go, giving the mind a rest, and detaching from seeking an immediate solution—that's all that's necessary. This clears the space for you to allow an answer in.

TRUSTING IT

Only four people survived above the 78th floor in the south tower of the World Trade Center on September 11th. They did it by acting against the advice of others and going down the stairs through smoke and debris. Dozens more, possibly hundreds, could have taken the same path to safety. Instead, they went up in search of a helicopter rescue that would never come. The story of Stairway A is a haunting exception to an otherwise successful evacuation.

FOUR SURVIVED BY IGNORING WORDS OF ADVICE

Faith, Not Fear

Impulses of thought communicate through your emotions, where your body always knows the truth. When we are afraid, we tend to tighten up and become what's commonly referred to as "being uptight." Making any decision from this place where you are not centered will never be in your best interest. Likewise, when you are in a state of worry, you are presetting a negative goal in your mind as to how it's going to turn out. To help you make a decision, do the following.

Take a piece of paper and draw a line down the center. Label the left column "Faith" and the right column "Fear." Write down all the thoughts that line up on each side in reference to your decision. In other words, write down any worries, risks, and costs in the "Fear" column, and write down any hopes, expectations, and benefits in the "Faith" column. Step away and come back to this page in a little while. Take an honest look—in which direction is your decision leaning? If the decision is primarily rooted in fear, consider another path. What results can potentially happen in the other column based on faith? Keep filling out both columns. This is a stream-of-consciousness exercise that taps into instinctual thoughts that will support you.

As a gutsy move, share this list with someone who cares about you, and ask if he or she sees the same outcomes that you see. Ask for any solutions that may blindside you because you're too close to the problem. The objective is to cross off all your fears and identify the reasons why you can and should remain in faith. Is there any truth to your fears, or are you projecting an experience that is manufactured in your mind? Are you fully expecting and imagining something negative to occur in the future as a result of this decision? Are you surrounded by well-meaning people who are pointing out more of the risks rather than benefits associated with your desired choice?

When you have a burning question that would help you make the next best decision, the solution never shows up at the same time. This is because, energetically, the question often comes from a place of lack or scarcity, where you want your solution right then and there. The answer, when it arrives, comes from a place of abundance, where you are in full expectation and faith. However, you can't find that state of allowing, unless you disconnect from the dilemma.

As an example, imagine that you have found your ideal home and are ready to buy the property. However, now you are unsure of whether you can afford it and doubt whether it's a sound financial decision that will support you in the future.

Steve

- **Faith.** I've been working for many years and saving; I can afford this. I easily make friends and form connections. This home is warm and inviting and will create a positive environment that will support me. It's in a location that will attract people who feel that way too if I wish to sell it one day. This home will propel me into being more successful because I've committed to investing in something that brings me joy. It feels good to commit to something and invest in me. I will surround myself with a community of new friendships that I can rely on.
- **Fear.** I could lose my job and be unable to make the mortgage payments. I won't be able to sell it later on. This is the largest purchase I've ever made. If something major breaks, I will lose my freedom to buy things that I enjoy. I don't know anyone in the neighborhood. I don't deserve a large property like this. I should downsize and save for the future. I may outgrow this house and then need to move again. Its market value can depreciate. This decision feels irresponsible.

If you act based on fear, how does that choice trickle down to other areas of your life? How likely would you jump on an opportunity to lead a presentation to a wider or senior audience in your industry or secure a new leadership role that you can grow into with hundreds of employees under your responsibility?

And most important, have the courage to follow your heart and intuition. They somehow already know what you truly want to become. Everything else is secondary.

STEVE JOBS

Steve Jobs gave this close in his commencement address in 2005 at Stanford University. Later it drew so much conjecture about what he meant that a full chapter was devoted to intuition in his biography, *Becoming Steve Jobs.*[1] On the surface, the concept appeared to translate to a "follow-your-passion" theme. Yet the authors argue that Steve's gut instinct looked very different before and after he established his corporate success:

> Early in his career, intuition had meant shuttered confidence in the inventions of his own brain. There was a stubborn refusal to consider the ideas of others. By 2005 intuition had come to mean a sense of what to do that grew out of entertaining a world of possibility. By then he was confident enough to listen to his team as well as his own thoughts and to acknowledge the nature of the world around him.[2]

Following through on your intuition steadily strengthens self-trust.

The Breakdown Before the Breakthrough

Sometimes life gets harder before it gets better. Have you ever experienced a string of random negative events that suddenly have the power to place your life on hold? If so, then you are all too familiar with the breakdown before the breakthrough. A sudden injury can stop you in your tracks, a relationship is tested, a colleague begins to overstep his or her boundaries—the list is endless. Random events and breakdowns begin to happen and leave you standing out in the cold wondering, "How did I create this?" There is something coming around the corner when you experience this sharp contrast that has placed you in the eye of a storm. Hold the line: a breakthrough is on its way.

Rather than resist, consider it a trial-and-tribulation period that you can trust, being called on to grow. We can't control events; they show up when they want. Your point of power is always in your response—following your instincts, taking action, leading from faith to create a new set of results. Even staying still in the eye of the storm is action as long as you are observing the shifts happening around you.

ALLOWING IT

Water Stimulates Energy

There are times when we freeze in the middle of a conversation with no rational explanation. We forget what we're about to say or simply go off on a tangent. We may be confident in what we know, but instead, we recognize that we're not establishing the best presence we can because of feelings of unworthiness that come to the surface out of nowhere.

When this freeze factor occurs, imagine yourself surrounded by water, gushing up high around and above you. Allow yourself to be grounded by the water; feel it touching your skin and protecting your body from your head to your toes; allow its protective force to keep you safe. Let go and enjoy the cool splashes on your face. Trust that your words will come; water has the power to recalibrate you to wellness.

If I asked you to imagine yourself standing on a sandy beach in front of an ocean, it likely wouldn't be too difficult. Visiting an ocean can evoke an overwhelming sense of exhilaration and joy. The thought of the warm sun shining over you, of your breathing in the fresh air and hearing the sound of waves gently rolling in, can have a power that goes beyond peaceful nostalgia. Everything about this scene may feel real, adding to a perfectly stimulating meditative experience. Water has a magnetic force, and science has studied whether it can, in fact, change the human brain wave frequency, slowing us down to a calmer state. You can find this same force field sitting by a lake with still water. Often believed to have a direct connection to a higher energy wave, water with its boundless energy holds the power to support you.

Our intuition is always speaking to us, and it is often impossible to hear in our day-to-day distracting world. We're often so focused on our external reality that our intuitive guidance system is pushed aside, even though it's continuously nudging us in the direction we need to go. Those are the impulses that come out of nowhere. Instinctual thoughts can happen in any setting, perhaps even while you drive down long stretches of open road. Tapping into this quiet force field doesn't take long, and you don't have to push so hard to get there. You were placed on earth with a guidance system. It's called your *gut instinct*, and it is designed to help you create a life that you love with joy. The only caveat is that you will face unwanted experiences along the way that are purposely placed there to allow you to choose. It's not until you mentally nod to the things you want and deserve that you eventually create those things and turn away from that which no longer serves you. Trusting your instincts is a split-second decision you can make daily. To demonstrate how simple this is, snap your fingers together right now. That was a waking moment to trust yourself.

Find Your Word

What is one word that you want to be, have, or experience? Maybe your word is *growth*, or *strength*, or *love*. Whatever you decide it is, you can't just know it. You have to *be* it and allow it to expand your life. Write your word on a small piece of paper. Every night before bed, take a glass of water and put it on top of your word. Let it sit overnight. The next morning, drink the water and think about how you will start that day with the intention of being that word in every way.

Define how that word will show up in your life. Work backward. If your closest friend were to come for a surprise visit three months from now, what would he or she see happening in your life? What would have to show up for you so that, without a doubt, another person could witness that you are *freedom*, or *hope*, or *peace*?

As humans, the act of getting up to do something is as natural as breathing. If someone were to ask you to go meditate on something or physically go work on it to create a new outcome, which of the two actions do you think you would likely choose? There is usually less resistance around doing, and this is why we tend to forget the being aspect as human beings ourselves.

Following your intuition is a two-step dance that combines thought with action. Before you set out to do something, you first need to eliminate resistance and any limiting beliefs that show up when you reach a perceived obstacle. Once that wall is down, you will receive the inspired thoughts and intuitive hits that will guide you to the next best course of action you should take. This is how you build confidence over time and learn to trust your instincts, establishing a stronger self-trust. You now have a stronger force field of energy supporting you. Note that you can't follow your instincts unless you're able to take your guard down and change your belief system. This is when you're ready to tune in and tap into your higher consciousness, often referred to as the *mind behind the mind*.

If action is needed, then follow the path of least resistance. You may choose to go out for a drive or a walk that feels good and inspires you to consider the next best thing you can do. But you wouldn't have gotten into the car in the first place if you weren't experiencing listlessness or restriction. So you felt the impulse to act and let go and do it. There wasn't any resistance around that or negative expectations from taking the much-needed drive. Now you're feeling better, and your body is moving, which can feel like excellent progress.

Now you follow the next inspired thought to call someone. That certain someone gives you some words of encouragement around your predicament. You are feeling better again. Now you may be in a better place to go on an interview or ask for something. What's important to note is that you weren't able to directly take that course of action without choosing to feel better by taking small incremental steps that silenced your mind. Energetically, you are at a higher frequency than you were before, and taking action, asking for things in your life at this time, will support you.

Doing deep breathing and closing your eyes are also effective at helping you tap into your intuition and create calm. This slows down the cycle of brain wave activity to an alpha state, much like when you are in the early stages of sleep yet still awake. Much of your alert and wakeful hours are in the beta state of cyclic brain movement.

Earlier, when you felt you had few options and your back was against the wall, there was too much resistance. However, now that you have calibrated and taken the time to rest and practice self-care, you have unlocked possibility and are open to what's coming with a core belief that whatever thoughts you have, they will benefit you. Owning your belief system is having an unwavering faith in yourself when you say *yes*.

Yes, you deserve happiness and success.

APPENDIX

BREAKTHROUGH TO SUCCESS: TAKE THE OWN YOUR AUTHORITY DEEP DIVE

If you are ready to own your authority in your career, join us for a positively motivating experience: take the self-study "Own Your Authority Deep Dive" online course or attend a live master class. Learn how to quickly increase your influence as a leader. The "Own Your Authority Deep Dive" is perfect if you are at the midcareer stage seeking more leadership or just a few years into your career having just stepped into a leadership role. It also works well if you are in an executive role and you need to stand out more, gain more influence, and move those planned initiatives forward. If you are considering a career transition, it will support you in seeking clarity on how to define this next exciting phase of your life.

Join us to remain committed to your goals and meet other professional leaders in your shoes. Your career leadership strategy goes beyond just transitioning to a new level of influence. It must support you staying there with resilience and remaining relevant. Learn more about available programs at OwnYourAuthorityBook.com.

101 WAYS TO OWN YOUR AUTHORITY: RECEIVE THE AUDIO COURSE AND REPORT

Sit back and listen to a complimentary audio course that is rich in practical information that can start working for you in your career, not based on theory or feel-good advice. It covers specific work scenarios from a list of 101 strategies you can implement quickly and without much effort, strengthening your instincts. The beauty of this list is that even if you only take action on 10 percent of these items, you will see results. Keep leaning into these daily instinctual triggers. The guidance shared here is based on years of real on-the-ground experience with what it really takes to get out there with courage, leading with an action plan and consistently reaching your goals strategically. You don't need to push hard whenever you feel stuck. It's about slaying the conversations in your mind that are negatively affecting the decisions you make in your career and life, gaining back your power, and owning your personal authority.

The success you desire is right around the corner for you. Don't let anyone (including you) convince you that you are not good enough. Because you have everything you need to get to the next level in your career. Download the report and listen to the leadership audio course at www.OwnYourAuthorityBook.com/101ways.

EMPOWER OTHERS TO TRUST IN THEMSELVES

The greatest gift you can give yourself is to cultivate your self-awareness. The more self-aware you are, the more clarity you gain on who you are and what you need in your relationships. It is the foundation of your personal growth.

I encourage you to share copies of this book with your college-age children, colleagues, team members, and managers and any leaders you know who are ready to maximize their potential and see themselves in a reflective and meaningful way. The words of empowerment and instinctive career strategies spelled out here can also open up an honest dialogue with other people, not to mention a lively exchange of stories you can share of lessons learned and committed actions you each can take in your own careers. Simply sharing out loud anything you intend to achieve can put the wheels in motion to realizing your goals. Visit www.OwnYourAuthorityBook.com and let us know what you will commit to in your career!

JOIN THE GUTSY LEADER MOVEMENT LIVING THE PRINCIPLES!

Beyond the career strategies spelled out here, the complete leadership curriculum in our leadership academy teaches success-growth strategies and life principles shown to create breakthrough results in your own, personal development that will impact your life. I envision a world where adults and children trust their instincts, face their fears, lead outside their comfort zones, and act in spite of difficult circumstances to realize their fullest potential. Whether you'd like to unleash one breakthrough goal, attend a writer's retreat, or teach others with a natural gift to empower those who seek your advice, join us and take a nonnegotiable approach in any area of life. Visit our programs at www.OwnYourAuthorityBook.com to learn more about joining our leadership academy.

EMPOWER THE LEADERS OF YOUR ORGANIZATION: KEYNOTE, WORKSHOP, WEBINAR, AND LEADERSHIP ACADEMY

Do your leaders need greater success in challenging and uncertain times? A leadership program in any format will naturally inspire and motivate participants to take on greater challenges, attract more opportunities, and produce breakthrough results in their careers. The leadership curriculum shows exactly how to plan for and create greater influence in your career. It's also a proven blueprint for living a life of expanded results, greater impact, and more measurable performance. It will help the people of your organization attract more opportunities, raise their influence and gain more recognition, create compelling stories that command attention, have more courage, expand their network, make meaningful connections, find more structure between work and family, and avoid bright shiny objects that take away their best time and energy. In this content-rich program, not only will participants leave inspired about their personal and professional potential, but they'll also create a clear personal plan of action. To learn more, go to www.InRShoes.com. More than just a motivational experience, this program offers actual methods, strategies, activities, and exercises that participants need to achieve their business goals—and what you as a value-driven company want for them!

NOTES

Introduction

1. Delivering through Diversity from McKinsey. https://www.mckinsey.com/~/media/mckinsey/business%20functions/organization/our%20insights/delivering%20through%20diversity/delivering-through-diversity_full-report.ashx.
2. Definition of latin proverb: https://en.wikipedia.org/wiki/Still_waters_run_deep#:~:text=Still%20waters%20run%20deep%20is,a%20passionate%20or%20subtle%20nature.

Chapter 1

1. https://www.ncbi.nlm.nih.gov/pmc/articles/PMC4685017/.
2. Pauline Clance and Suzanne Imes, "The Impostor Phenomenon Among High-Achieving Women: Dynamics and Therapeutic Intervention." *Psychotherapy Theory, Research, and Practice* 1978; 15(3):241–247.
3. Bradley A. Hanson and Thomas W. Harrell, "Predictors of Business Success Over Two Decades: An MBA Longitudinal Study." Working Paper No. 788, Stanford Graduate School of Business, 1985.

Chapter 2

1. Napoleon Hill, *Think and Grow Rich*, TarcherPerigee, 2005, p. 245.

Chapter 3

1. Philip S. Clifford, Bill Lindstaedt, Jennifer A. Hobin, and Cynthia. N. Fuhrmann, "Opportunities Come Through People," *Science*, July 16, 2013, www.sciencemag.org/careers/2013/07/opportunities-come-through-people.

Chapter 4

1. Marianne Williamson, *A Year of Miracles: Daily Devotions and Reflections*, HarperOne, 2015, p. 1.
2. Ralph Keyes, *The Writer's Book of Hope: Getting from Frustration to Publication*, Holt Paperbacks, 2003, p. 107.
3. James Egan, *Over 100 Ways to Stop Sabotaging Your Life*, lulu.com, 2015, p. 50.
4. Paul Mercer, *Babe Ruth (Sports Heroes & Legends)*, Barnes & Noble, 2003, p. 60.
5. Joseph McBride, Steven Spielberg: A Biography, Second Edition, University Press of Mississippi, 2011, p. 131.

6. Esther Hicks and Jerry Hicks, *Ask and It Is Given: Learning to Manifest Your Desires*, New York: Penguin Random House, 2004.
7. Ed Yong, "Justice Is Served, but More So After Lunch: How Food-Breaks Sway the Decisions of Judges," *Not Exactly Rocket Science*, April 11, 2011, www.discovermagazine.com/the-sciences/justice-is-served-but-more-so-after-lunch-how-food-breaks-sway-the-decisions-of-judges.
8. Hicks and Hicks, *Ask and It Is Given*, p. 331.
9. Gail Matthews, https://scholar.dominican.edu/cgi/viewcontent.cgi?article=1265&context=news-releases.
10. This experience was sourced from the "Do Something Principle" described by author Mark Manson in his article at https://markmanson.net/how-to-get-motivated#action.

Chapter 5

1. Interview with Frank Sinatra, https://www.youtube.com/watch?v=Y-xkTDhOpCY.

Chapter 6

1. Brent Schlender and Rick Tetzeli, *Becoming Steve Jobs: The Evolution of a Reckless Upstart into a Visionary Leader,* Stanford, 2015, Chapter 13.
2. Ibid.

INDEX

ABOUT THE AUTHOR

MARISA SANTORO is a motivational speaker, corporate leadership trainer, diversity and inclusion consultant, and career coach. Her expertise in leadership and professional development, as well as effective business communication, has been brought in to support business leaders across industries such as American Express, UBS, Anheuser-Busch, Allianz Global Investors, Sony Music, S&P Global, Royal Bank of Canada (RBC), Aetna Healthcare, New York University (NYU), NYU Langone Medical Center, and many more.

Marisa is a former Wall Street IT executive with a two-decade career in Financial Services, a TEDx speaker, and honoree of the Woman of Influence award from *New York Business Journal* and bizwomen.com for her years of mentoring and coaching midcareer leaders, executives, healthcare professionals, and sales leaders to achieve higher levels of influence.

Marisa is the CEO and founder of the career platform In Our Shoes (www.InRShoes.com) and the professional development online school and community Gutsy Leadership Academy (GLA). *Own Your Authority* (www.OwnYourAuthorityBook.com) is based on the success growth principles found in the curricula of all her leadership programs.

She is also a national career columnist at *American City Business Journals (ACBJ)* covering their how-to career and business strategy sections, with articles published across 44 cities in the United States.

Marisa received her MS from New York University's Stern School of Business and Courant Institute of Mathematical Sciences and her BA from Pace University, Seidenberg School of Computer Science and Information Systems.

She lives in the New York City region with her other half, Vince, and two junior gutsy leaders, Isabelle and Julien.